THE REFUGEES FROM SLAVERY

IN CANADA WEST.

REPORT

TO THE

Freedmen's Inquiry Commission,

BY

S. G. HOWE.

BOSTON:
WRIGHT & POTTER, PRINTERS, 4 SPRING LANE.
1864.

PREFACE.

During the last summer, the United States Freedmen's Inquiry Commission made an investigation, through one of its members, of the condition of the colored population of Canada West.

This pamphlet contains the result of inquiries and observations made during the investigation. At any time but this, an apology might be necessary for putting forth, in such a hasty and crude form, the observations and speculations which it contains. But now, when every body is asking what shall be done with the negroes,—and many are afraid that they cannot take care of themselves if left alone,—an account of the manner in which twenty thousand are taking care of themselves in Canada, may be interesting, even if it be imperfect, and contain superfluous speculations.

It is commonly said that the Canadian refugees are "picked men;" that the very fact of their escape from slavery, is proof of their superiority; and therefore, however well they may succeed in taking care of themselves, it does not prove that ordinary negroes can do the same. There is more point than force in this. In the first place, there are vast regions of slave territory, from which escape to Canada is almost impossible. Secondly, men may lack the courage and skill which are necessary to insure escape from slavery, but possess all the qualities necessary to provide for themselves and their families.

The local attachments of the slaves are very strong. They cling far more fondly than whites do to the "old place." They want to be free; and have a strong, though vague feeling, that freedom will, somehow, and at some time, come to them. Some are restrained from flight by moral qualities which are in themselves excellent. They fondly love their families. They often have personal and tender attachment to their masters, and more often to his children and family. They have a feeling of loyalty, and shrink from the idea of betraying trust. Others again are restrained by a feeling of religious obligation, having been taught Scripture in such garbled and distorted form, as to make them believe it enjoins obedience to masters, even if obedience leads to all manner of sin. Finally, it is the testimony of intelligent men from the Slave States, who know the Canadian refugees, that they are fair representatives of the colored population, free and slave, of the Border and Middle States.

No! the refugees in Canada earn a living, and gather property; they marry and respect women; they build churches, and send their children to schools; they improve in manners and morals,—not because they are "picked men," but simply because they are *free men*. Each of them may say, as millions will soon say,—"When I was a *slave*, I spake as a slave, I understood as a *slave*, I thought as a *slave;* but when I became a *free man*, I put away slavish things."

The writer desires to express his thanks for the kind and courteous manner in which gentlemen, in various parts of Canada, endeavored to facilitate my inquiries. All were civil and kind; but Messrs. Thomas Henning and McGann, of Toronto; Dr. Litchfield, of Kingston; Rev. Hiram Wilson and Dr. Mack, of St. Catherines; Rev. Mr. King, of Buxton; Mr. McCullum and Mr. Wm. H. Howard, of Hamilton; Dr. A. T. Jones and Mr. Thomas Webb, of London; Mr. J. W. Sparks, of Chatham, were very useful.

But he would especially acknowledge his obligation to Mr. J. M. W. Yerrinton, Secretary of the Commission, who accompanied him as Reporter, and who, by uncommon intelligence and tact, assisted in gathering a great deal of valuable information. This is added to the large body of evidence concerning the condition of the colored people in various parts of the United States, gathered by the Freedmen's Inquiry Commission, and will be given with their final Report.

S. G. H.

Boston, *December* 31, 1863.

Messrs. Robert Dale Owen *and* James McKaye,

Of the Freedmen's Inquiry Commission:

Gentlemen,—The undersigned respectfully asks leave to make through you, to the Secretary of War, the following Report of his observations of the condition of the colored people of Canada West.

The fact that many thousands of blacks and mulattoes, who have fled from slavery, or from social oppression in this country, are living in Upper Canada as free men, with all the rights and privileges of British subjects, is too important to be overlooked by a Commission of Inquiry into the condition and capacity of the colored population of the United States, just set free.

These emigrants, or rather exiles, are fair representatives of our colored people. They are in about the same proportion of pure Africans, half-breeds, quarter-breeds, octoroons, and of others in whom the dark shade grows fainter and fainter, until it lingers in the finger-nails alone. The greater part have been slaves, or are the children of slaves; but many were born free, of free parents. They have been, during many years, in about the same condition as that in which our newly-freed people now find themselves. They have been trying the experiment, for their race, of their capacity for self-support and self-guidance, under the ægis of the law, indeed, but amidst an unsympathizing population, just as our freedmen are about to do.

It became very desirable, therefore, to learn the history, condition, and prospects of the colored population of Canada, in view of the light which might be thrown upon the general subject which the Commission is to investigate. But this could not be done without personal inspection and careful study. The undersigned, therefore, with your consent, undertook this, and proceeded to Canada, in company with Mr. J. M. W. Yerrinton, Secretary and Reporter of the Commission.

We visited all the large towns, in which the colored population exist in considerable numbers, St. Catherines, Hamilton, London, Toronto, Chatham, Buxton, Windsor, Malden, Colchester, and spent in each all the time necessary to get a good idea of the people. We inspected many small settlements and detached farms, occupied by colored people. We saw the mayors and city officials in most of the cities, the sheriffs, jailers, constables, the schoolmasters and the clergy, and took their testimony. We also saw and conversed with a great many colored people at their houses, shops and farms.

The testimony of all these persons was taken down carefully, word for word, and is preserved. Some of it will be introduced into this Report;—more, indeed, of that given by refugees than may at first seem called for; but it is to be considered that all the influences which formerly acted upon them, and moulded their character, have been until within a few months acting upon the colored population, whose condition and prospects the Commission is to study.

The negro, like other men, naturally desires to live in the light of truth; but he hides in the shadow of falsehood, more or less deeply, according as his safety or welfare seems to require it. Other things equal, the freer a people, the more truthful; and only the perfectly free and fearless are perfectly truthful.

Already the negroes in Canada show the effect of freedom and of fearlessness.

"I served twenty-five years in slavery," testifies William Grose, "and about five I have been free. I feel now like a man, while before I felt more as though I were but a brute. When in the United States, if a white man spoke to me, I would feel frightened, whether I were in the right or wrong; but now it is quite a different thing: if a white man speaks to me, I can look him right in the eyes,—if he were to insult me, I could give him an answer. I have the rights and privileges of any other man. I am now living with my wife and children, and doing very well."*

Said David West, a man of religious character:—

"I myself was treated well in slavery. I hired my time, and paid my master two hundred dollars a year, but my master died, and I heard that I was to be sold, which would separate me from my family, and knowing no law which would defend me, I concluded to come away. * * * * * * *

"I have known slaves to be hungry, but when their master asked them if they had enough, they would, through fear, say 'Yes.' So if asked if they wish to be free, they will say 'No.' I knew a case where there was a division of between fifty and sixty slaves among heirs, one of whom intended to set free her part. So, wishing to consult them, she asked of such and such ones, if they would like to be free, and they all said 'No:'—for if they had said yes, and had then fallen to the other heirs, they would be sold,—and so they said 'No,' against their own consciences. But there will be a time when all will be judged."†

* The Refugee, or Narratives of Fugitive Slaves in Canada, by Benjamin Drew.

† Ibid.

While, therefore, the testimony of negroes in Canada must be taken with due allowance for liability to error and disposition to exaggerate, it must not be considered as testimony taken from the same class of persons in the Southern States would be. There the negroes are held to be untruthful, almost as a matter of course. In Canada, they are not. In the South, they have motives for lying which do not affect them in Canada; for, in the latter, it is evident that they have the most entire reliance upon the protection which the law gives them. Complain as they may about other matters, they all admit that; and it is a common remark with them, that they are not now afraid to say things that are true, for "the law will bear them out in it."

Said Leonard Harrod:—

"A man can get more information in Canada about slavery, than he can in the South. There I would have told you to ask master, because I would have been afraid to trust a white man: I would have been afraid that you would tell my master. Many a time my master has told me things to try me. Among others, he said he thought of moving up to Cincinnati, and asked me if I did not want to go. I would tell him, 'No! I do n't want to go to none of your *free* countries!' Then he 'd laugh,—but I did want to come—surely I did. A colored man tells the truth here,—there he is afraid to."*

The testimony of these refugees was given with simplicity and apparent honesty. It was given by persons not connected with each other; and mostly by persons not acquainted with each other. Taken as a whole, and sustained by the testimony collected from over a hundred

* Drew, p. 340.

refugees, by Mr. Drew, several years ago, it bears strong internal evidence of truth. It is a fearful record of the meanness, the vices and the crimes into which men are apt to be drawn, when they are wicked enough, or weak enough, to commit the folly and sin of holding their fellow-men as slaves.

From the information thus gathered, from all sorts of men, the undersigned endeavored to form a just opinion of the material, moral and social condition of the colored people of Canada West.

He endeavored, moreover, to gather the statistics of population, of property, of crime, of mortality, and the like. This was difficult, because the law does not recognize distinction of color, and the official records do not show it, except in the prison returns. For instance, the roll of tax-payers does not distinguish between whites and blacks; but the local officers generally know every individual, and by their assistance, which was generally rendered very cheerfully, the exact number of colored tax-payers, the amount of their tax, and the comparative amount paid by blacks and whites, in several places, were ascertained.

With this statement of the object of the inquiry, and of the sources of information, the undersigned proceeds to report the result of his observations and thoughts upon this remarkable emigration, under the following heads:—

First. The history of the emigration, its causes, its progress, and the actual number of the emigrants.

Second. The physical condition of the emigrants, as affected by climate, soil, intermarriage, and the like.

Third. Their material condition, as shown by their

property, taxes, pauperism, and the appearance of their houses and farms.

Fourth. Their mental and moral condition, as shown by the general character they bear, the condition of their schools, churches, societies, and their mode of life.

Fifth. General inferences, to be drawn from the experience of the colored people in Canada, as to the future condition of those in the United States.

Liberty will be taken to enlarge upon such matters as seem to throw any light upon the difficult problems which must soon be solved in the United States, by reason of the important changes in the legal and social condition of so many of its inhabitants.

Section 1.—*History.*

Canada has not been long a place of refuge for the oppressed. The Indians, imitating our pious ancestors, stole or bought negroes, and held them as slaves. Sophia Pooley, who was living very recently, though over ninety, says:—

"I was stolen from my parents when I was seven years old, and brought to Canada; that was long before the American Revolution. There were hardly any white people in Canada then—nothing here but Indians and wild beasts. Many a deer I have helped catch on the lakes in a canoe: I was a woman grown when the first governor of Canada came from England: that was Governor Simcoe.

"My parents were slaves in New York State. My master's sons-in-law, Daniel Outwaters and Simon Knox, came into the garden where my sister and I were playing among the currant bushes, tied their handkerchiefs over our mouths, carried us to a vessel, put us in the hold, and sailed up the river. I know not how far nor how long—it was dark there all the time. Then we came by land. I remember when we came to Genesee, —there were Indian settlements there,—Onondagas, Senecas, and Oneidas. I guess I was the first colored girl brought into Canada. The white men sold us at Niagara to old Indian Brant, the king. I lived with old Brant about twelve or thirteen years, as nigh as I can tell. Brant lived part of the time at Mohawk, part at Ancaster, part at Preston, then called Lower Block: the Upper Block was at Snyder's Mills. While I lived with old Brant, we caught the deer. It was at Dundas, at the outlet. We would let the hounds loose, and when we heard them bark, we would run for the canoe—Peggy, and Mary, and Katy—Brant's daughters and I. Brant's sons, Joseph and Jacob, would wait on the shore to kill the deer when we fetched him in.

"King Brant's third wife, my mistress, was a barbarous creature. She could talk English, but she would not. She would tell me in Indian to do things, and then hit me with any thing that came to hand, because I did not understand her. I have a scar on my head, from a wound she gave me with a hatchet; and this long scar over my eye is where she cut me with a knife. * * * * Brant was very angry, when he came home, at what she had done, and punished her as if she had been a child. Said he, 'You know I adopted her as one of the family, and now you are trying to put all the work on her.'

"I liked the Indians pretty well in their place; some of them were very savage, some friendly. I have seen them have the war dance, in a ring, with only a cloth about them, and painted up. They did not look ridiculous; they looked savage—enough to frighten any body. One would take a bowl, and rub the edge with a knotted stick; then they would raise their tomahawks and whoop. Brant had two colored men for slaves; one of them was the father of John Patten, who lives over yonder; the other called himself Simon Ganseville. There was but one other Indian that I knew who owned a slave. I had no care to get my freedom.

"At twenty years old, I was sold by Brant to an Englishman in Ancaster, for one hundred dollars. His name was Samuel

Hatt, and I lived with him seven years; then the white people said I was free, and put me up to running away. He did not stop me; he said he could not take the law into his own hands. Then I lived in what is now Waterloo. I married Robert Pooley, a black man. He ran away with a white woman; he is dead."*

The French tolerated the "Institution." There are sad monuments of the barbarous system still standing. At Malden, you may see "the bloody tree" used as a whipping-post for slaves. The English, when they seized Canada, not only tolerated the existing system of slavery, but expressly provided for importing negroes from Africa and elsewhere, by an Act in the thirtieth year of George III., "for encouraging new settlers in his Majesty's Colonies and Plantations in North America." By virtue of this Act, negroes were imported and held as slaves. It is a remarkable fact, that some escaped from their masters and fled to the United States, to enjoy freedom there. A case of this kind was related to us by Mrs. Amy Martin. She says:—

"My father's name was James Ford. He was born in Virginia, but was sold to Kentucky, and was there taken by the Indians. He was eighty-six years old when he died, and would be over one hundred years old, if he were now living. The Indians brought my father to Canada—I think to Fort Malden. He was held here by the Indians as a slave, and sold, I think he said, to a British officer, who was a very cruel master, and he escaped from him, and came to Ohio. He got off in a sail-boat, and came to Cleveland, I believe, first, and made his way from there to Erie, where he settled. After I came over here, I married a man who was also a fugitive, and the old folks moved over here to be with me in their old age. When we were in Erie, we lived a little way out of the village, and our house was

* Drew, p. 192.

a place of refuge for fugitives—a station of the underground railroad. Sometimes there would be thirteen or fourteen fugitives at our place. My parents used to do a great deal towards helping them on to Canada. They were sometimes pursued by their masters, and often advertised; and their masters would come right to Erie. We used to be pretty careful, and never got into any trouble on that account, that I know of. The fugitives would be told to come to our house."

The act of thirtieth George III. was in full and binding force until July 9, 1793. Then the Provincial Government declared as follows: "That whereas it is unjust that a people who enjoy freedom by law should encourage the introduction of slaves, and whereas it is highly expedient to abolish slavery in this Province so far as the same may gradually be done *without violating private property*," &c., therefore the authority "to grant license for importing any negro or negroes into this Province is hereby repealed."

The 2d section provided that nothing in the Act should extend to contracts already made.

The 3d section provided that children born of female slaves, *after* the passage of the Act, should remain in the service of the owner of the mother until twenty-five years of age, when they should be discharged. It further provided for registration of births, and penalties for neglecting the same.

Section 4th provided remedies against undue detention of such persons beyond the age of twenty-five: also for the freedom of children born to them while under twenty-five years of age.

Section 5th provided for security to be given by masters liberating their slaves, that such persons should not be chargeable to the public; but no part of the Act provided for the freedom of any slave born before July 9, 1793; nor has any subsequent Colonial legislation done it.

Nothing in this Act affected the status of any negro slave born previous to the date of it. On the contrary, the 2d section provides that nothing in it shall disturb existing relations. The legislation was prospective merely; and there has been none subsequently. Therefore a slave born before July 1, 1793, would have been legally a slave until the general abolition of slavery in all the British colonies by act of Parliament in 1833. Thus slavery had a legal existence in Canada many years after it had been abolished in several States of the United States.

Massachusetts abolished it by her Bill of Rights in 1780; New Hampshire in 1792; New York in 1799; New Jersey in 1820; and it was virtually abolished in the other Northern States before 1830.

But though the Canadian Parliament, with the usual veneration of legislators for things hallowed by age, merely scotched slavery, public opinion (and the cold) would not let it drag out its legal life, but killed it before the beginning of this century.

For several years, the existence of freedom in Canada did not affect slavery in the United States. Now and then a slave was intelligent and bold enough to cross the vast forest between the Ohio and the Lakes, and find a refuge beyond them. Such cases, however, were, at first, very rare, and knowledge of them was confined to few; but they increased, early in this century; and the rumor gradually spread among the slaves of the Southern States, that there was, far away under the north star, a land where the flag of the Union did not float; where the law declared all men free and equal; where the people respected the law, and the government, if need be, enforced it.

The distance was great; the path difficult and dangerous; and the land, instead of milk and honey, abounded in snow and ice. It was hardly a place in which white men could live, much less black men; who, moreover, were told monstrous stories about it, in order to deter them from fleeing thither.

"After we began to hear about Canada," said J. Lindsey, "our master used to tell us all manner of stories about what a dreadful place it was; and we believed some of them, but some we didn't. When they told us that we must pay half of our wages to the Queen, every day, it didn't seem strange nor wrong; but when they said it was so cold there that men going mowing had to break the ice with their scythes, I didn't believe that, because it was onreasonable. I knew grass wouldn't grow where ice was all the time." "I was told before I left Virginia," said Dan Fackart, "I have heard it as common talk, that the wild geese were so common in Canada, that they would scratch a man's eyes out; that corn wouldn't grow there, nor any thing else but rice; that every thing they had there was imported."

Nothing invited the negroes to this cold region, except the still small voice of Freedom; but some of them heard and answered that. They braved the imaginary dangers, overcame the real ones; and many found that resolute and industrious men, even if black, could live and enjoy the rights of men in Canada.

Some, not content with personal freedom and happiness, went secretly back to their old homes, and brought away their wives and children at much peril and cost.

The rumor widened; the fugitives so increased, that a secret pathway, since called the underground railroad, was soon formed, which ran by the huts of blacks in the Slave States, and the houses of good Samaritans in the Free States; and they placed by its borders helps which the wayfarer could find, even in the night. Hundreds trod this path every year, but they did not attract much public notice.

The slaves have always instinctively felt that the enemies of our country must be their friends, and that war time was good time for them. Consequently, they improved the opportunity of the war of 1812–14, and escaped into Mexico and Canada. The loss of "property" became so great in the following years, that in 1826, Mr. Clay, Secretary of State, instructed Mr. Gallatin, our Minister to St. James, to propose to the British Government a stipulation for "*a mutual surrender of all persons held to service or labor, under the laws of either party, who escape into the territory of the other.*"

"Our object," said the Secretary, "is to provide for a growing evil."

Early in 1827, he again called Mr. Gallatin's attention to the matter, informing him that a treaty had been negotiated with Mexico, by which she had engaged to return our "runaway slaves."* The Minister was to press upon the British government the importance of the stipulations about mutual surrender, in view of the danger of the escape of slaves from the West India Islands to our shores. Thus the great Republic was not only to change

* The treaty was negotiated, but the Mexican Senate refused to confirm it.—*Jay's View.*

its fundamental policy of being a place of refuge for all the oppressed, but try to shut up such places elsewhere.

In July of the same year, Mr. Gallatin communicated the manly conclusion of the British government, that "*it was utterly impossible for them to agree to a stipulation for the surrender of fugitive slaves.*"

But the power behind the White House, which ever directed the national policy in the interests of slavery, persisted in its purpose.

On the tenth of May, 1828, a resolution was passed the United States House of Representatives, *without a division of the House*, "*requesting the President to open a negotiation with the British government in the view to obtain an arrangement whereby fugitive slaves, who have taken refuge in the Canadian Provinces of that government, may be surrendered by the functionaries thereof, to their masters, upon their making satisfactory proof of their ownership of said slaves.*"

June 13, 1828, Mr. Clay transmitted this resolution to our new Minister, and again spoke of the evil "as a growing one, well calculated to disturb the good neighborhood which we are desirous of cultivating with the adjacent British Provinces."

Eager to seize their prey, the slaveholders could not brook diplomatic delay, but at the very next session procured the passage of a resolve calling on the President to communicate the result of the negotiation; and he showed that he had been swift to run before their wishes, by sending in a mass of documents bearing upon the subject.

The result of the negotiation was, as Mr. Barbour, our

new Minister, wrote October 2d, 1828, that Lord Aberdeen insisted "*that the law of Parliament gave freedom to every slave who effected his landing upon British ground.*"*

Thus the Monarchy rebuked the Republic; spurned the proposal of a mutual betrayal of exiles, and assured the sanctity of the Canadian asylum to fugitive slaves.

Meantime, free colored people, mulattoes, offspring of negroes and whites, were multiplying rapidly, and spreading over the whole Union. These half-breeds, if not equal to the whites in mental force, were not stupid, nor lazy, but thrifty and shrewd; and they prospered in worldly things. Their prosperity begat the desire of security for their freedom, which they could not have in the South; and for social rights, which they could not have, either in the North or South. The barbarous legislation, in some of the so-called free States, bore very hardly upon these people. Therefore, they too began to look to Canada as a place of refuge.† This gave another impetus to the emigration.

Meantime, the steady progress of the slave power toward complete domination of the whole land culminated in the passage of the Fugitive Slave Bill. This opened all the United States to slave hunters, and put in peril the liberty of every one who had even the faintest tinge of negro blood. Of course it gave great increase to the emigration, and free-born blacks fled with the slaves from

* State Papers 1827-8, Vol. 1, Doc. 19.

† "Owing, among other causes, to the extremes of climate in the more northern States, and in other States to expulsive enactments of the Legislatures, the free colored show a decrease of numbers during the past ten years according to the census, in the following ten States."—*U. S. Census, Prelim. Rep.*, '60, p. 6.

a land in which their birthright of freedom was no longer secure.*

Such is a brief outline of the general causes and history of the remarkable exodus of colored people from the United States.

It is impossible to ascertain the number of exiles who have found refuge in Canada since 1800; but according to the most careful estimates, it must be between thirty and forty thousand.

It is difficult, moreover, to ascertain the present number. The census of 1850 is confused. It puts the number in Upper Canada at 2,502 males, and 2,167 females.† But in a note it is stated, "*there are about* 8,000 *colored persons in Western Canada.*‡ This word *about* is an admission of the uncertainty; and, as if to make that uncertainty greater, the same census in another part puts the number in Western Canada at 4,669.§

The abstract of the census of 1860 makes the colored population to be only 11,223. Doubtless, in some districts, the distinction between colored and whites was not made. At any rate, the number is greatly under-stated, because in several cities, the records show that there must be a greater number than is given in the census. For instance, in St.

. . . * "New York has increased from 3,097,394 to 3,880,735, exhibiting an augmentation of 783,341 inhabitants, being at the rate of 25.29 per cent. The free colored population has fallen off 64 since 1850, a diminution to be accounted for probably by the operation of the *fugitive slave law*, which induced many colored persons to migrate *further North.*"—*U. S. Census*, '60, *Prelim. Rep.*, p. 4.

† See Census Report of the Canadas, 1850, Vol. 1., p. 317.

‡ Ibid., Vol. 1., p. 37.

§ Ibid., Vol. 2., p. 3.

Catherines, C. P. Camp, Town Clerk, said to us:—"*The Government Census is all wrong (about our place). They made the population* 6,284 *by last Census; but we took the Census a year ago and made it* 7,007."

Indeed, the town records show that there are 112 colored tax payers! In the Government School, the attendance of colored children in winter is from 130 to 140. About forty were attending one private school. The inference from these data would be that the colored population is, as was represented to us by Elder Perry and others, about 700. The Census makes it only 472!

In Hamilton are three colored churches, two of which we attended. The colored population is probably over 500, but the Census makes it only 62!

In Toronto, Mr. George A. Barber, Secretary of the Board of School Trustees, furnished us a certified copy of the number of colored residents, amounting to 934, but the Census makes it only 510.

The Mayor of London, C. W., estimated the number of *families* among the colored people at 75, but the Census makes the whole colored population only 36!

There has been no movement of the colored population sufficient to explain such discrepancies, and the conclusion is that the Census of 1850, and that of 1860, included some of the colored people in the white column.

The report of the Anti-Slavery Society of Toronto, in 1852, estimated the colored population of Canada West at 30,000.

Intelligent people, acquainted with the matter, estimate the present population at from 20,000 to 30,000. Our own calculation is, that it does not fall short of 15,000, nor exceed 20,000.*

However imperfect these latter estimates may be, it is evident, from the number known to have entered Canada, that the births have never equalled the deaths, and therefore, there has been no natural increase, but on the contrary, a natural loss; and that without constant immigration, the colored population must diminish and soon disappear.

Section 2.—*Physical Condition, &c.*

Most of the colored people of Canada were born in the United States. In order, therefore, to understand their physical character, we should look to the stock whence they sprang, and to the changes wrought upon it by a colder climate and new mode of life.

The proportion of pure Africans among the colored people of the United States is very small indeed. Even upon the Southern plantations they are rare. Those imported from Africa are soon affected in their appearance, especially in that of the skin, by the climate and by slave life; and their direct descendants, owing to mixture of individuals from different tribes, rapidly lose their tribal peculiarities. But their direct descendants are comparatively few; the mulattoes, offspring of the cross between negroes and whites, are more numerous, and they, of course, depart more widely from the original type.

During the early period of our history, Africans, mainly Congoes, were landed all along the Atlantic

* See Appendix, Note 1.

coast. The importation into the Northern Colonies was never large; it soon grew less, and ceased entirely before the close of the last century; while the importation into the Southern regions, always larger, was kept up longer; and some have been smuggled in within a very few years.

The crossing with the white race immediately began every where, and although it did not last long in the North, it has been kept up vigorously in the South to the present time.

From this crossing of races came that mulattoism, which, unfortunately, is so wide spread among the whole population of the United States, and which impairs the purity of the national blood, taken as a whole.

Now, the condition of the Canadian emigrants, who are mostly mulattoes, goes to confirm what besides is a natural inference, that if this evil had not been fostered by social influences, it would have been checked, and in time, cured.

This certainly could have been done, because the mulattoes of the United States are not a race, but a breed; and breeds are produced, modified, and may be made to disappear, by social agencies. Proofs of the potency of these agencies abound. The careful observer will find them in the demand and supply, and in the geographical distribution of the productions of the breeding States. Different kinds of colored men are demanded, and the supply meets the demand. Slender, light-built quadroons, or octoroons, are wanted for domestic purposes; dark and heavier men for the field. Black women are wanted for their strength and fruitfulness; yellow ones for their beauty and comparative barrenness. If they are not wanted where they are raised, they are taken to the proper market. Henry Clay did not like to testify against "the institution," yet he said, in a speech before the Kentucky Colonization Society, in 1829: "It is believed that nowhere in the farming portion of the United States would slave labor be generally employed, if the proprietors were not tempted to raise slaves by the high price of the southern markets, which keeps it up in their own." The consciousness of any purpose in all this may be indignantly repelled; but the commercial laws act; and there are those who study them, and trade upon them, as much as the breeders of cattle do. The proofs of this are abundant.

Thus commercial interests disturb, to a certain extent, the natural laws; for there is in the social system, as in the individual body, a recuperative principle which tends to bring men back to the normal condition of their race. No purely natural causes could have multiplied and perpetuated such a breed in such a climate as ours. On the contrary, there is reason to think that the offspring of the cross between the small number of pure Africans formerly slaves in the Northern States and the whites would have dwindled, and by this time nearly disappeared, by reason of the effect of climate, of further crossing between half-breeds, and their comparative infecundity, but for continual accessions from the South. There, in a more favorable climate, a fruitfulness greater than follows intercourse between mulattoes was and is kept up, by constant crossing with the white race.

From this central source in the South, then, comes the

flood of adulterated blood, which spreads, whitening a little as it flows, but which reaches the North, and helps to retain there the taint which was fast vanishing.

Statistics carefully kept in some Northern cities, where mulattoes intermarry among themselves, and where crossing with whites is not common, show that births among colored people are less numerous than the deaths! But in the South, the affinities of race, the partial infecundity of hybrids, and other natural causes which tend to purify the national blood, are counteracted by social causes, among which is the market value of the offspring; in other words, the premium set upon hybrids.

At the beginning of this century, the total number of colored people in the United States was 1,002,798, of whom 109,194 were free; and in 1860, it reached 4,435,709, of whom 482,122 were free.

They have spread over most of the country, the density of their population, and the darkness of their complexions, diminishing northward.

From this population came the colored people of Canada, who are mainly of two classes, slaves who escaped from bondage or freed men who fled from social oppression in the Slave States, and free men who were driven by social oppression, and iniquitous legislation, from the Free States.

Taken as a whole, they resemble in physical aspect the colored people of the Middle States rather than those of the extreme Southern, or the extreme Northern States. They present about the same proportion of blacks and mulattoes, shading off to white.

They are slightly built, narrow-chested, light-limbed, and do not abound in thews and sinews. They are mostly of lymphatic temperament, and show strong marks of scrofulous or strumous disposition. This is discernable in the pulpy appearance of certain parts of the face and neck; in the spongy gums, and glistering teeth.

They are peculiarly disposed to the sort of diseases to which persons of this temperament are most liable; and the climate makes the development of such diseases more certain. The children are subject to mesenteric and other glandular diseases. The young are liable to softening of tubercles; and there is a general prevalence of phthisical diseases.

The most reliable medical opinions are that these people are unfavorably affected by the climate.

If, indeed, one should consider only the opinion and testimony of the people themselves, he would conclude that they bear the climate very well, and are as healthy and as prolific as the whites. But the opinion of the common inhabitants of any place respecting its salubrity is often not worth much. They who give it, find themselves alive and well; they see a few old men and women about, and expect to grow old like them; their neighbors are alive and well; the sick are out of sight, and the dead out of mind.

If we seek the focus of any plague or epidemic, common people are apt to tell us that it is not in their precise locality; it is "over yonder" in some other place; or if there be a few victims in their town, they must be strangers and unacclimated persons; or, at worst, those who had peculiar dispositions to that particular disease, of which disposition they themselves do not partake.

So the colored people of Canada say the climate suits them; that they are very well; that they bear as many children as whites do, and rear them as well. But the opinion of the most intelligent white persons is different.

Many intelligent physicians who have practised among both classes, say that the colored people are feebly organized; that the scrofulous temperament prevails among them; that the climate tends to development of tuberculous diseases; that they are unprolific and short-lived.

From an abundance of such testimony, the following, given by two eminent physicians, one in the West, the other in the eastern part of Upper Canada, is selected as among the most reliable. Dr. Fisher, physician at the Provincial Lunatic Asylum, says:—

"I think the colored people stand the climate very badly. In a very short time lung disease is developed, and they go by phthisis. The majority do not pass forty years. Of course, there are exceptions. They die off fast. I suppose I have had thirty colored people here with little children, with scrofulous disease, extending as far as ulceration of the temporal bone. Then they are a good deal subject to rheumatism. They bear a great many children, but raise only about one-half of them, I think. The children are generally weakly and puny; not so strong as our white children. A great many of them die in childhood. The principal disease is tubercular deposition of the stomach and intestines."

Dr. T. Mack, of St. Catherines, says:—

"It strikes me that the mixed races are the most unhealthy, and the pure blacks the least so. The disease they suffer most from is pulmonary — more than general tubercular; and where there is not real tubercular affection of the lungs, there are bronchitis and pulmonary affections. I have the idea that they die out when mixed, and that this climate will completely efface them. I think the pure blacks will live. I have come to this conclusion, not from any statistics, but from personal observation. I know A, B, and C, who are mulattoes, and they are unhealthy; and I know pure blacks, who do not suffer from disease, and recover from the smallpox, and skin diseases, and yellow fever, which are very fatal to mulattoes. I think there is a great deal of strumous diathesis developed in the mixed race, produced by change of climate."

The vital statistics of the colored people in Canada have not been kept with sufficient accuracy by the official authorities to warrant any conclusions; but they have been kept in some parts of the Northern States where the climatic influences are at least as unfavorable as those of Canada.

Take, for instance, the following extract from the report of the Registrar of the City of Boston:—

"The following table will present, in an interesting form, the number of births, marriages and deaths among the colored population in each of the last eight years:

YEAR.	Births.	Marriages.	Deaths.
1855,	29	35	63
1856,	50	46	71
1857,	34	34	73
1858,	24	32	60
1859,	46	37	58
1860,	29	53	68
1861,	47	41	60
1862,	45	38	47
Totals,	304	316	500

"It will be noticed, that in each of the years named, the colored deaths exceeded the births; and that in 1855, 1858 and 1860, the latter were even less than the marriages! During the whole period, the deaths exceeded the births by nearly two hundred, and the marriages by twelve. Estimating the white population at 180,000, the proportion of births to the whole number is as one to 34.50; while the ratio of colored births is as one to 49, in a population of 2,200. It is not the less interesting to observe, that while this difference in the natural growth of the two races is so strikingly in favor of the white, the marriages among the colored race were in the ratio of one to 58 of the population, while among the former they were only as one to 87.54!

"Thus it is shown, that in each of the aspects in which this subject may be viewed, the colored race seems, so far as this city is concerned, to be doomed to extinction."

J. R. Bartlett, Secretary of State for Rhode Island, commenting on the State Registration Reports, says:—

"These Reports illustrate the peculiarities of the colored race, as it exists in this State. Rhode Island has had a higher proportion of colored persons than any other New England State. This proportion is lessening from year to year, *in spite of a slight and concealed current of immigration* from Southern States. The mortality of the colored is about twice as great, in proportion, as that among the white. In a period of nearly five years, the deaths of colored persons have been fifty-seven more than the births of colored children."*

The Seventh Registration Report says: "The colored race would at no distant day become extinct in Rhode Island, if it were not maintained by immigration."†

Col. (now General) Tullock, and Staff Surgeon Balfour,

* 5th Registration Report, State of Rhode Island, pp. 47, 48.

† 7th Report, p. 64.

of the British Army, published four volumes of military statistics, between 1848 and 1851, which are admitted to be very valuable.

The first, in a MS. letter dated November 25, 1863, says :—

"It was shown by reference to the mortality among the slave population in Jamaica and the West Indies, for a series of years, that when not recruited by fresh importations, that race would probably become extinct in little more than a century; an anticipation which is now, I believe, in the course of being realized, except on the Island of Barbadoes.

"The annual mortality of the negroes averaged, at that time, about three per cent. among the male population of all ages in these colonies; it was still higher in the Mauritius, as also in the French settlements of Bourbon, Martinique, Guyana, and Senegal. You are aware that with so high a mortality among persons of all ages, it was impossible for any race materially to increase, or even to keep up its numbers, especially as a further extension of the inquiry showed that this loss fell chiefly on the adult population; children under ten years of age being usually as healthy as those of English parentage in this country. In illustration of the loss among these adults, even under the most favorable circumstances, I pointed out that in the West India Regiments and Black Pioneers, men between the ages of twenty and forty-five, the loss was usually four per cent. in the West Indies, three per cent. in Jamaica, and that even on the west coast of Africa, the latter rate prevailed, while in the Mauritius, among a similar class, it rose to nearly four per cent., and still higher in Ceylon and Gibralter, where negro troops were for a short time employed.

"This high mortality among the negro race was found chiefly to arise from their extreme susceptibility to diseases of the lungs; indeed, it will be seen by the returns of total diseases annexed to the volumes just referred to, that as many died from them alone, as from all other diseases; so far as my experience goes, no race has ever shown less adaptability for a variety of climates. In the Southern States of America alone does there appear a fair prospect of their being able to increase and keep up their numbers, probably in consequence of the climate being favorable to those diseases by which they are elsewhere most affected.

"With regard to the mulatto race, I have few facts to offer, because, as a general rule, they are seldom employed in our army; chiefly owing to *the want of that physical stamina* which renders the pure negro better fitted for the duties of a soldier or a laborer. So far as I am aware, our colonies possess no separate records of the mortality to which mulattoes are subject, but in some of the French Colonies before referred to, where the distinction has been kept up, the death rate appears to be a medium between that of the negro and the naturalized white settler. If a fair comparison could be drawn from the rate among the Eurasian or half castes in India, it would be decidedly unfavorable to the longevity of the mixed race, as it is very rarely that any are found to arrive at a third generation."

Dr. Andrew Fisher, of Malden, Canada, says:—

"I should say that mulattoes don't have children enough to keep up the breed without assistance from emigration, from the fact that more of the diseases I have been mentioning, [phthysis, scrofula and rheumatism,] are developed among mulattoes than among pure blacks."

Such statistics and such opinions confirm the conclusion, drawn from other sources, that without the continuance of mulatto breeding in the South, and fresh accessions of population from that quarter, mulattoes would soon diminish in Canada; and, moreover, that mulattoism would fade out from the blood of the Northern States.

Upon the whole, then, the colored population of Canada, considered solely in a physical light, is a poor one. They are of a breed which is neither vigorous nor prolific; and though in its present phase it seems to evolve considerable vivacity of temperament and activity of intellect, its tendency is rather to deteriorate than improve.

The offspring of the cross show less ferocity than their progenitors, certainly than their white ones ; but this is perhaps from diminished intensity and virility of their whole nature. The animal organism is less intense in its action. The mulatto, considered in his animal nature, lacks the *innervation* and *spring* of the pure blacks and whites ; or, is less "high strung." The organic inferiority is shown in less power of resisting destructive agencies ; in less fecundity, and less longevity.

Now, that this is not solely the result of unfavorable climatic influences in Canada and New England, is shown by the vital statistics of Liberia. There is the native country of the negro. There, if any where, he should flourish. That Colony is made up of precisely the same class of emigrant-freed negroes, mostly from the border States, and mostly mulattoes. The first emigrants were sent there forty years ago ; and up to January, 1858, eleven thousand one hundred and seventy-two had been landed. A very few have returned; and yet, with all the fostering care of the Societies, and with all the aid and appliances that kindness and money could afford, "the colonists, with all their natural increase, numbered only 7,621 in 1858!"* A loss by excess of deaths over births of 33 per cent! The Haytian emigration has been equally disastrous.

The unfavorable peculiarities of the cross breed are

* "Liberia As I Saw It," by Rev. A. M. Cowan, Agent Kentucky Colonization Society, p. 166.

perhaps increased in the Canadian emigrants by intermarriage within too small a circle.

If slavery is utterly abolished in the United States, no more colored people will emigrate to Canada; and most of those now there will soon leave it. There can be no doubt about this. Among hundreds who spoke about it, only one dissented from the strong expression of desire to "go home." In their belief, too, they agreed with Rev. Mr. Kinnard, one of their clergy, who said to us, "if freedom is established in the United States, there will be one great black streak, reaching from here to the uttermost parts of the South."

Or, if slavery is only so maimed and crippled that it can no longer affect the freedom of the dwellers in the Northern States, there will be no further emigration to Canada. Refugees from slavery will not cross the lakes, but remain in the Free States. Those now in Canada will disappear by a slower process; for, as was just said, when the fecundity of mulattoes is not increased by occasional return to one of the original types, it rapidly lessens, at least on this continent above the thirty-fifth parallel of north latitude.

But, if slavery is neither abolished in the South, nor prevented from encroaching upon personal freedom and security in the North, then the colored population of Canada, like that of the Northern and Western States, will go on increasing, as it has done, not by its own inherent fertility, but by immigration from the border and Southern States, where intercourse between the purer types of each race is frequent, and where increase is encouraged by the *marketable value of the offspring.*

In connection with the physical condition of the exiles, it may be as well to consider here the subject of

Amalgamation of Races.

It is feared by some that emancipation, by breaking down certain barriers between the white and black races, may greatly increase their amalgamation. The Canadian experiment may throw some light upon this matter.

During many years, the refugees were mostly men; and to this day, the males are most numerous, because women cannot so easily escape. Now, the consequence of any departure from the natural numerical proportion between the sexes must of course be bad; and the wider the departure, the greater the evil becomes, until it culminates in the morbid tastes and monstrous abominations engendered in communities made up of one sex only. Natural tastes and dispositions, unduly thwarted, are perverted into morbid and monstrous passions. If uncultured black men cannot find black mates, they will find white ones, and the contrary.

It appears that formerly, that is, in the early period of the emigration, marriages, or open cohabitation, between black men and white women, were not uncommon. The marriages were mostly with Irish, or other foreign women The instances of white men openly cohabiting with black women were very rare; and marriages of this kind were too uncommon to need notice.

Dr. Litchfield, medical superintendent of criminal lunatics, says: —

"It is not uncommon here for a colored tradesman to marry a white woman. The stipendiary magistrate of Kingston enumerated some ten or twelve colored men in this locality who had married white women. These women were generally Irish women, from the class of domestics."

It is to be remarked that Kingston is far removed from the region most populated by colored people; and that probably the first colored emigrants were chiefly *men*.

Within twenty or thirty years, many men have contrived to redeem by money, or by pluck and enterprise, their former wives or sweethearts. Slave women, too, heard about Canada, and learned the way. Other colored women came in from the Northern and Western States, so that the numerical disparity between the sexes soon began to lessen, and continues to do so. This of course tended to check amalgamation with whites.

Meanwhile, another corrective, and that the most important of all, began to be felt. As soon as the disturbing forces of slavery and social oppression ceased to act, the negroes, true to human instincts, began to be drawn together by more natural affinities than existed between them and another race. They grouped themselves into families, and sanctified them by marriage.

Bishop Green, a colored man of the Methodist Episcopal Church, says:—

"There is not much intermarriage between the colors. But our people have too much good sense to think a white woman is degraded because she marries a black man. A respectable colored man and a respectable white woman are looked upon as a respectable family. The people don't say any thing against such marriages. If the man is an upright man, and the woman an upright woman, they treat them as if they were both colored; they have sociability among them. Here is Mrs. ———, the wife of a colored grocery-keeper, who is held in as much respect among the first colored women as any black woman in town. Here is Mrs. ———. Her husband is a house-plasterer, and she is as much respected as any white woman. I don't know that there are more such cases now than formerly. *The most of them marry in the States, and move here.* The immediate community here have their associations with their own people, and you *do not see any of our respectable people here marrying any persons but their own associates.* The young men of our community are of opinion that they can find as good wives among their own class as can be found any where, and you can't find any of them offering to marry a white woman. They have their own associates, I assure you, and they cannot be influenced to do otherwise. These intermarriages are exceptional cases. Most all of them are from the States."

Other colored men take a less liberal view of the matter than does the kind-hearted Bishop. Says John Kinney, a very intelligent man,—

"The majority of the colored people don't like the intermarriage of colored and white people. I want to have a woman I am not ashamed to go into the street or into company with, and that people won't make remarks about. It don't amount to any thing, I know, but it hurts a man's feelings."

Col. Stephenson, who has had much acquaintance with colored people, and who employs many of them, says:—

"They do n't marry much with whites; it is looked upon with such dreadful contempt by all classes—even by the negroes themselves. The respectable colored people do n't like to have one of their color marry a white woman."

Mayor Cross, of Chatham, says:—

"They do not intermarry much with the whites, and it is only the most abandoned whites who marry them. It is a very good trait in the character of the people, that they do not regard it as any honor to marry a white person. A very laughable incident occurred here the other day. A colored man ran away with a white girl, and another colored man, speaking of the affair, said: 'I always looked upon him as a respectable man. I did n't think he would fall so low as to marry a white girl.' "

Dr. Fisher, in whose neighborhood is a very large colored population, says:—

"Those who are here generally marry among themselves, and keep aloof. I have been here four years, and I have never heard of a white person getting married to a colored one."

Mr. Sinclair, teacher of the public school of Chatham, says:—

"So it is with a white woman who marries a negro. The whites will have nothing to say to her, and her society is entirely with the blacks. Such marriages occur once in a while, but not so frequently as they did a number of years ago. There was considerable stir and fuss made about it, and the greater part of the colored people, and their leading men, are opposed to it themselves."

Thus the desire to imitate the higher civilization around them, seconded by the influence of the church, has brought the colored people rapidly up, and out of their loose and incontinent habits. The refugees, when living among those of their own color, and able to earn a livelihood, follow the attraction of natural affinities, eschew marriage with whites, and build up families among themselves. White men will not marry black women; and notwithstanding the fearful social pressure which often forces white women to venture upon any forlorn hope in marriage, few venture upon the most forlorn hope of all, in the present state of society—union with a black man.

Upon the whole, then, the experience of the Canadian refugees goes to show that there need be no anxiety upon the score of amalgamation of races in the United States. With freedom, and protection of their legal rights; with an open field for industry, and opportunities for mental and moral culture, colored people will not seek relationship with whites, but will follow their natural affinities, and marry among themselves. With the additional advantage which they will, or surely ought to have, of choosing the soil and climate most congenial to their nature, they will give no trouble upon this score, at least in the Northern, Western or Middle States. Drawn by natural attractions to warmer regions, they will co-operate powerfully with the whites from the North in re-organizing the industry of the South; but they will dwindle and gradually disappear from the peoples of this continent, outstripped by more vigorous competitors in the struggle for life. But, surely, history will record their blameless life as a people; their patient endurance of suffering and of wrong; and their sublime return of good for evil to the race of their oppressors.

SECTION 3.—*Material Condition—Property, Taxes, &c.*

Has the negro the ability and the will, to work and support himself, in a state of freedom?

Many anxious souls are now pondering this question, just as if it had not been solved, over and over again.

In the South, especially in the Border States, thousands of slaveholders show their faith by their actions; for they leave the negro to lead and direct the field hands, to manage their small farms, and to run their mills; they send him to neighboring markets to sell garden stuff, and to more distant markets with droves of hogs and cattle; and they even confide to him small craft, with their cargoes, on rivers and lakes. But especially does that large class believe, who *hire him out to himself*, by the month or year, and ask not and care not what he does, so that he pays them punctually for the use of his own brain and muscles.

Again, there are about a half million* free colored people in the United States, who not only support themselves, with less aid from public charity than our foreign population receive, but contribute to the material prosperity of the country. Of these, there are 225,955 in the Slave States, and 262,015 in the Free States. The former, notwithstanding they are unenfranchised, and labor under various political and legal disabilities, support themselves and contribute to the general weal.

In Maryland, for instance, according to the Preliminary Report of the U. S. Census, 1860, "This class, constituting as it does, 12 1-4 per cent. of the whole population, forms an important element in the free labor of the State."†

In Kentucky, they support themselves, build churches, live in neat and comfortable houses, pay taxes, and are respectable and useful inhabitants.

In Louisiana, and in other States, many of them are wealthy. Those in the Free States, in spite of blind and

* 487,970—Abstract U. S. Census, 1860, p. 3.

† Abstract U. S. Census, 1860, p. 6.

bitter prejudice, are thriving; as the abundant testimony gathered by your Commission, will prove.

Still, many people are made to believe that the negro is too lazy to work, except under compulsion. To such, the Canadian experiment may furnish another line and precept.

Let it be borne in mind, however, that the refugees find no other advantage in Canada except freedom and protection by the laws. In all other respects, they labor under very great disadvantages. Chiefest is that of

Climate.

This is even a greater obstacle than appears at first, for it is a feeble breed, and not a vigorous race, which has to resist its rigors. Forced to flee their own country, they were thwarted at the very outset, in a very important matter; because considerations about warmth are always leading ones in the choice of new dwelling-places. Men instinctively seek the temperature best suited to their organization. Long residence even, in a country the temperature of which is not congenial to a race, does not change their disposition; and if they make a voluntary emigration, its track will be along the isothermal line native to their fathers. As a geologist who finds a fragment of an early stratum above a later one, infers that it must have been rent from its connection by some convulsion, so the sociologist who finds people of African descent, living in an arctic region, infers that it must have been driven, not drawn, thither. If free to choose their own dwelling-places, the negroes would be surely drawn by thermal laws, from the Northern and Western States, and towards the tropics. But slavery reverses even physical laws, and drives men who would fain live where the lizard can bask all the year round, to a region in which the fox and deer can hardly resist the bitter cold.

It is true that the refugees are not generally conscious of the great disadvantage of the climate. Indeed, to hear them talk, one would suppose they were "to the arctic born." They have a bravado way about it, and say, "We can stand the climate just as well as white men,"—unconscious of the import of the words "*stand a climate!*" that is, contend with it as with an enemy; fight against it; keep up a life-long struggle with it, and expend their energy in retaining the warmth of which it is continually robbing them.

Now and then one, of happy organization, like the jovial watchmaker, Sparks, at Chatham, seems to thrive on cold. "I like it, first rate," said he; "I weighed only 179 pounds when I came here, and now I weigh 241." And his shadow is not becoming less.

All the facts, however, are against the theory of their becoming acclimated; and some of the most thoughtful ones among them are aware of it. The following are selected from the testimony; and they are the words of men whose natural ability and acquired knowledge would make them remarkable in the industrial ranks of any community.

Alfred Butler, of Toronto, says:—

"Our people find the climate here pretty tough for the first winters, but we get used to it after a while. Of course, it does not agree with us so well as a warmer climate would. I don't think it quite so easy to raise children here as down South. I think the climate preys more upon the constitution than the Southern climate does. I have become pretty well acclimated here, and I can endure as much cold as most people raised here; and yet I think the weather preys upon a person's constitution more, and a man gives way."

F. G. Simpson, of the same place, says:—

"I think, as a whole, the climate is rather too hard for the generality of the colored people—more especially those from the far South—though they stand it pretty well. But I notice that many of them die of decline or consumption here." * * "This climate is very changeable. I have seen it change twenty degrees in a few hours. Those not prepared with clothing suffer from these sudden changes. I doubt if our people are so fertile here as at the South. I think a warm country, for any race of people, tends to make them more prolific than a cold climate. I may be mistaken, but I don't think the colored people are so prolific here as they are in the States. Judging from appearances, there are not so many children here."

Says Dr. A. T. Jones, of London:—

"I do not believe the climate is altogether congenial with the health of the colored people. I do not think the colored community would flourish as much here as down in Kentucky or Maryland."

But a still greater disadvantage is that of

The Prejudice of the Whites against Negroes.

Peoples have their way of gossiping, just as individuals have; and a favorite one is that of criticising their neighbors, and talking national scandal. The American people are charged with prejudice against the negroes; and our English cousins especially denounce it as a proof of our innate depravity; while the more philosophic French smile at it as merely a proof of our being "behinded;" that is, less liberal than the "grand nation."

The affinity between all members of the human family which fits them for sympathy and affection is of course greater between proximate races than between remote ones. If a lone Caucasian in a desert should meet a Carib, (who did not happen to be hungry or angry,) they would probably be drawn together as brother men. If an African should come along, the Caucasian would prefer him by reason of closer affinity of race, and the Carib might complain of this as prejudice. A Mongol might wean the Caucasian from the African; but one of his own race would have still better chance for his sympathy. Even among the varieties of race, there are different degrees of natural affinity; and an Anglo-Saxon is drawn to a Teuton more readily than to a Celt. Now, this law of affinity is strong enough in a state of freedom to preserve the harmony of nature, and keep all men in their places; and if we add culture, all women too. The essentials, however, are freedom and culture; for without these the natural affinities will not prevent men warring upon each other, at small provocations; though never as they war upon wolves and other brutes. But because a man's sympathies with those of his own race are so strong that he cannot think of marrying into another race, and cannot think with pleasure of his child doing so, must this be charged as guilty prejudice? Does preference imply prejudice, any more than love implies hate? However, let the rationale of prejudice against the negroes be what it may, it surely does not become the English to reproach the Americans, as a people, with the sin of it; for they themselves have quite as much of it; and their people show it whenever the negroes come among them in sufficient numbers to compete for the means of living, and for civil rights. Whenever circumstances call it forth among the coarse and brutal, they manifest it just as brutally as Americans do. They have done so in Canada; and would doubtless do so in England.

If the French people are, as they boast to be, above this prejudice, (which is improbable,) it must be because they have greater moral culture, (which is more improbable;) or else that the Celtic element in their blood has closer affinity with the African than ours has.

The English Canadians try to persuade themselves that when this malady of prejudice does occasionally appear among them, they do not have it in the natural way, but catch it from the Americans; and that it breaks out in its worst form in towns where Americans most abound.

The Rev. Mr. Proudfoot, of London, is a friend of the colored people, and has shown his friendship by manly opposition to the popular cry for expelling their children from the public schools and putting them in separate schools. He said to us:—

"The prejudice against colored people is growing here. But it is not a British feeling; it does not spring from our people, but *from your people coming over here*. There are many Americans here, and great deference is paid to their feelings. * * * We have a great deal of Northern feeling here. The sympathy for the North is much greater than you would imagine. In fact, I have been very much vexed at it."

This opinion is hugged by very intelligent English people; and even such an enlightened man as Dr. Ryerson, Superintendent of Public Instruction, holds on to it. Said he to us:—

"The *American feeling* still exists in this country in regard to people of color, especially among the country people. I do not consider it a natural feeling, because it is not an English feeling."

The colored people, however, say, that this theory of contagion is not sustained by facts; and the bulk of the evidence shows that they are right.

The truth of the matter seems to be that, as long as the colored people form a very small proportion of the population, and are dependent, they receive protection and favors; but when they increase, and compete with the laboring class for a living, and especially when they begin to aspire to social equality, they cease to be "interesting negroes," and become "niggers."

The words of Mr. Meigs, of Malden, expressed the truth; but the contemptuous tone in which he uttered the last sentence, gave it additional force. Said he:—

"I have been here for twenty-three years. The feeling against the colored people has been growing ever since I came here, and more particularly since your President's Proclamation. They are becoming now so very haughty that they are *looking upon themselves as the equals of the whites!*"

This prejudice exists so generally in Canada, that travellers usually form an unpleasant and unjust opinion of the colored refugees, because it is usually strong and bitter in that class of persons with whom travellers come most in contact. For instance, the head-clerk in the ——— hotel at ———, in answer to our inquiries about the condition of the colored people, broke out as follows:—

"Niggers are a damned nuisance. They keep men of means away from the place. This town has got the name of 'Nigger

Town,' and men of wealth won't come here. I never knew one of them that would not steal, though they never steal any thing of any great amount. Chickens have to roost high about here, I tell you. The Grand Jury of this county has just indicted seven persons, and every one of them was black. They will steal a little sugar, or a pound of butter, and put it in their pockets. But perhaps they are not to blame for it, for they have been trained to steal in slavery."

This sort of evidence forms the staple out of which newspaper reporters manufacture articles, and form the public opinion about the Canadian refugees. Now, in this very hotel, the head waiter, an intelligent man, who enjoyed the respect and confidence of the household, clerks included, was a colored man—one who bought himself for $1,000, saving, with singular persistency and resolution, $50 a year for twenty years, for that purpose. His place was one of considerable consequence, requiring capacity and integrity; and he seemed to fill it to general satisfaction.

It is not, however, hotel clerks alone, but grave officials, Mayors and others, who, when first addressed, are apt to speak contemptuously of the colored people; though they usually do them more justice upon reflection; especially in those cities where the negro vote is large enough to turn an election.

The following is a fair sample of the matter of several of these conversations. After explaining our mission, and telling Mr. ——, head magistrate of ——, that the object of the interview was to ask his opinion of the colored people of his city, he said sharply:—

"Then my opinion is that niggers are a low, miserable set of people, and I wish they were not here."

"Well, let us see; are they intemperate?" "Oh, no; I must say they are not. Indeed, you never see any drunken negroes about."

"Are they riotous and ungovernable?"

"Oh, no, quite the contrary; none of our people are more easily governed, or give less trouble to the police."

"Are they much given to crime?"

"Yes, I think they are."

"More so than any other immigrants of the laboring class?"

"As to that, if you compare them with foreigners, they are not worse. They do steal chickens, and commit such petty offences, but then a great many white people do that, you know."

"Do they work and get their own living, or do they beg and depend upon public charity?"

"Negroes are too lazy to work hard; but I must admit that they are industrious. They keep pottering about, and pick up a good living, somehow. At any rate, they do not beg, and they have very few paupers."

"Well, if they don't get drunk, and don't steal over much, and don't beg, and don't become a public charge, and if they work and support themselves, why are they not good citizens?"

"I can't deny there's something in that. But still, I think they are a nuisance; I wish they were out of the place. I don't wish, however, to be quoted publicly as saying this, because, you know, it might make trouble."*

The Hon. Isaac Buchanan, M. P., of Hamilton, said to us:—

"I think we see the effects of slavery here very plainly. The children of the colored people go to the public schools, but a great many of the white parents object to it, though their children do not, that I know of. I suppose, if the question was put to vote, the people would vote against having the negroes remain here."

* Coarse people in Canada say "nigger" habitually; highly cultivated people, never. Others say "colored people," "negroes," or "niggers," according to their mood of mind.

Hon. George Brown, M. P., of Toronto, said:—

"I think the prejudice against the colored people is stronger here than in the States. To show you the prejudice that exists against them, I will mention one fact. When I was a candidate for Parliament in Upper Canada, 150 people signed a paper, saying that if I would agree to urge the passage of a law that the negro should be excluded from the common schools, and putting a head-tax upon those coming into the country, they would all vote for me; otherwise they would vote for my opponent. There were 150 men degraded enough to sign such a paper and send it to me."

Mr. McCullum, principal teacher of the Hamilton High School, says:—

"Up at the oil springs, the colored people have quite a little town. The white people were there, and they had all the work. They charged six shillings for sawing a cord of wood. The colored people went up there from Chatham, and, in order to get constant employment, they charged only fifty cents a cord. What did the white people do? They raised a mob, went one night and burned every shanty that belonged to a colored person, and drove them off entirely. Well, it was a mob; it was not society at all; it was but the dregs of society who did this. They took a quantity of the oil, and while some of their number were parleying with the colored people in front of their doors, they went behind, threw the oil over their shanties, set it on fire, and the buildings were in flames in a moment. The parties were arrested, and two of them sent to the penitentiary for seven years."

Rev. James Proudfoot, of London, says:—

"You will find a great many colored people about Chatham—too many. It has produced a certain reaction among the white people there. The white people do not associate much with them; and even in the courts of justice, a place is allotted to the colored people — they are not allowed to mix with the whites. A number of gentlemen have told me that."

Mayor Cross, of Chatham, says:—

"The colored people generally live apart. There has been, hitherto, a very strong prejudice against them, and the result is that they are, generally speaking, confined to a particular locality of the town."

Rev. Mr. Geddes, of Toronto, says:—

"The great mass of the colored population will be found in the West; and where they go in any great numbers, the people acquire a strong prejudice against them."

Mr. Sinclair, of Chatham, says:—

"Our laws know nothing about creed, color, or nationality. If foreign-born, when they take the oath of allegiance, they are the same as natives. But in regard to social prejudice, that is something we cannot help. The colored people are considered inferior, and must remain so for many years, perhaps forever, because their color distinguishes them. One or two colored men are constables here, but that is all." * * * *

"Many of the colored people, even in this town, say that if they could have the same privileges in the States that they have here, they would not remain a moment. The prejudice is not so strong in this town, where they have been so long known, and where the people see they can be improved and elevated; but even in this county, there is one township where no colored man is allowed to settle. One man has tried to build a house there, but as fast as he built it in the day time, the white people would pull it down at night. No personal violence was done to him. That was in the township of Orford. In the township of Howard, I think there are only four colored families, and they are a very respectable class of people. In that township, there was as much prejudice as anywhere, fourteen years ago; but two colored families, very respectable and intelligent people, settled there—they were rather superior in those respects to the neighborhood generally—and they did a vast amount towards doing away with the prejudice. They were intelligent, cleanly, moral, and even religious; so that ministers of the gospel would actually call and take dinner with these people, as they found every thing so nice, tidy and comfortable, and the poor colored people so kind, and so ready to welcome any decent person who came. So that a good deal depends upon the first samples that go into a town."

The testimony of the colored people is still more striking. Mrs. ——— Brown, (colored,) of St. Catherines, says:—

"I find more prejudice here than I did in York State. When I was at home, I could go anywhere; but here, my goodness! you get an insult on every side. But the colored people have their rights before the law; that is the only thing that has kept me here."

Dr. A. T. Jones, (colored,) of London, says:—

"There is a mean prejudice here that is not to be found in the States, though the Northern States are pretty bad."

Rev. L. C. Chambers, (colored,) of St. Catherines, says:

"The prejudice here against the colored people is stronger, a great deal, than it is in Massachusetts. Since I have been in the country, I went to a church one Sabbath, and the sexton asked me, 'What do you want here to-day?' I said, 'Is there not to be service here to-day?' He said, 'Yes, but we do n't want any niggers here.' I said, 'You are mistaken in the man. I am not a "nigger," but a negro.'"

Mrs. Susan Boggs, (colored,) of St. Catherines, says:—

"If it was not for the Queen's law, we would be mobbed here, and we could not stay in this house. The prejudice is a great deal worse here than it is in the States."

G. F. Simpson, (colored,) of Toronto, says:—

"I must say that, leaving the law out of the question, I find that prejudice here is equally strong as on the other side. The law is the only thing that sustains us in this country."

John Shipton, (colored,) of London, says:—

"I never experienced near the prejudice down there, (in the States,) that I have here. The prejudice here would be a heap worse than in the States, if it was not that the law keeps it down."

It would be easy to show how the natural sympathy and compassion which is felt for the exiles on their first arrival by all, and which continues to be felt by people of Christian culture, is converted into antipathy and animosity among the vulgar. The teachers in the pulpit, and the teachers of public schools, have much to answer for in this matter. The clergy of the Church of England are generally staunch friends of the negro. Rev. Mr. Geddes, of Hamilton, said:—

"There are several colored people belonging to my church. I have them also in the Sunday school, and have always taken an interest in the improvement of their condition, socially and religiously. There are two young colored women also in the Sunday school, who teach white children of respectable parents."

He related to us a case of two young ladies who were sent to Hamilton for education, and who joined his Sunday school. Their parents, on learning that colored children attended the school, sent a remonstrance, saying that their children must not be associated with negroes. His answer was:—

"I am sorry that any persons belonging to the Church of England are so narrow-minded as to suppose their children will be injured because there are a few colored persons in the same school; but of course we cannot change our principle, and the young ladies must leave."

Many Presbyterian clergymen are equally humane

and just; but there are those of all denominations who refrain from rebuking by their example the intolerant and unchristian spirit which prevails among their people.

So some of the teachers in public schools, rising to the dignity of their high calling, see in their colored pupils poor and friendless children, who have most need of sympathy and encouragement, and therefore they bestow them freely, careless whether committee-men and the public approve or not.

Mr. McCullum, principal of the well-appointed High School in Hamilton, says:—

"I had charge of the Provincial Model School at Toronto for over ten years, and I have had charge of this school over four years, and have had colored children under my charge all that time. They conduct themselves with the strictest propriety, and I have never known an occasion where the white children have had any difficulty with them on account of color. At first, when any new ones came, *I used to go out with them in the playground myself, and play with them specially*, just to show that I made no distinction whatever; and then the children made none. I found this plan most healthy in its operation.

"Little white children do not show the slightest repugnance to playing with the colored children, or coming in contact with them. I never knew of a case. But sometimes parents will not let their children sit at the same desk with a colored child. The origin of the difficulty is not being treated like other children. We have no difficulty here. We give the children their seats according to their credit-marks in the preceding month, and I never have had the slightest difficulty. The moral conduct of the colored children is just as good as that of the others."

In London, the head-master of the High School manifested a different spirit: he said,—

"It does not work well with us to have colored children in school with the whites. In our community, there is more prejudice against the colored people, and the children receive it from their parents. The colored children must feel it, for the white children refuse to play with them in the playground. Whether it is a natural feeling or not I cannot tell, but it shows itself in the playground and in the class-room."

One of the teachers said:—

"I think that the colored children would be better educated, and that it would be more conducive to the happiness both of colored and white children if they were in separate schools. The colored children would not be subjected to so much annoyance. Some white children of the *lower orders* don't mind sitting by them in school; but there are others who are very particular, and don't like it at all."

Now, this head-master is a man of vigorous nature, who makes his influence felt widely; and should he exert that influence as Mr. McCullum does, then perhaps "*it would work well* to have colored children in school with the whites;" then perhaps his sub-teachers would not show such lack of sympathy with the little colored children committed, in the providence of God, to their charge; then perhaps there would be no such sad sight as we saw in the playground, where colored children stood aside, and looked wishfully at groups of whites playing games from which they were excluded. Such scenes do not occur in the playground at Hamilton, because the teacher takes care, by showing *personal interest* in the colored children, to elevate them in the eyes of their comrades. Moreover, it is not likely that the school committee of London would persist in efforts to expel colored children from the public schools, and so degrade them in the public eye, if one humane master should publicly protest against it, as any citizen has a right to do.

Toronto and Hamilton are distinguished among the populous places of Canada West for the comparative liberality and kindness towards colored people. London is not; and the difference arises in some degree, doubtless, from the different spirit which children imbibe in the public schools under different head masters. At any rate, this accounts for the difference better than the theory of "contagion" from Americans does.

The Canadians constantly boast that their laws know no difference of color; that they make blacks eligible to offices, and protect all their rights; and the refugees constantly admit that it is so. The very frequency of the assertion and of the admission, proves that it is not considered a matter of course that simple justice should be done. People do not boast that the law protects white men.

After making all due allowance for the fact that the lack of culture disqualifies most of the refugees for many offices to which they are legally eligible, and also for refined society, there is manifest injustice done to them in various ways by reason of a vulgar and bitter prejudice, which defeats the benevolent purposes of the law. For instance, they are practically kept off the juries. The testimony of Mr. A. Bartlett, town clerk of Windsor, shows one way in which it is done. He says:—

"The selection of the jury is a simple thing. We begin with the man who is assessed the highest on the roll, and we go down to half the names on the roll; then the amount paid by that person who is lowest on the first half forms the amount of property qualification for that jury. Then we take two-thirds of that number, and of course the selectors have it in their power to say what two-thirds shall be taken; and of course the colored man is cut off, because they don't want him on."

It happens sometimes that a sturdy Englishman, seeing only his duty, insists upon its being done legally and impartially, and then colored men are drawn.

Such a case happened recently. A black man was drawn and duly summoned. He appeared in court, and was placed upon the jury, to the consternation of some snobs, who refused to sit in the box with him. The Judge had the manliness to reprimand them, then to fine them, and finally to imprison them; which at last brought them to what senses they had.

There is the same practical difficulty with regard to

Public Schools.

The Canadian law makes no distinction of color. It proposes that common schools shall be beneficial to all classes alike. Practically, however, there is a distinction of color, and negroes do not have equal advantage from public instruction with whites. The law allows colored people to send their children to the common schools, or to have separate schools of their own. They have asked for and obtained such separate schools in Chatham, Malden, and Windsor. Now, there is a growing feeling among the whites that they made a mistake in giving the blacks their choice; and a strong disposition is manifested in many places to retract it, and to confine colored children to separate or caste schools.

On the other hand, there is a growing feeling on the part of the colored people that they made a mistake in asking for separate schools; and a strong disposition is manifested to give them up; but the whites will not allow them to do so.

This again shows how surely the natural sympathy for the refugee is converted into antipathy or prejudice whenever, by increase in number, they come into antagonism with the dominant class. By such antagonism, the natural affinities between the whites become intensified, and they desire to keep the blacks in a separate caste, because they feel that it must be a lower one. Many colored people see this also, and they desire to prevent the establishment of such caste. Each party begins to see that the democratic tendency of the common school is to prevent or weaken castes, while the inevitable tendency of the separate schools is to create and to strengthen them.

The struggle has already commenced in several places. The school committee of London has shown its purpose of removing the colored children from the common school to a separate school *; and the colored people have declared their purpose of resisting it. Most active among them is Dr. A. T. Jones, a very black man, and a very intelligent one also; although he was a slave during the first twenty years of his life. He testified as follows:—

"The people here won't make the separate schools go. When they try it, they will have trouble. I will tell you precisely what I tell them. I tell them—'I have eight children, who were all born in this town,—British subjects, as much as the whitest among you; and they don't believe in any thing else but the Queen. Now, instead of leaving these children to

* See Report of a Sub-Committee of the School Trustees of the City of London; in appendix No. 2. It is valuable, inasmuch as it shows how illiberal and unjust well-meaning men may become when governed by the spirit of caste.

grow up with that love for the country and the Queen, you are trying to plant within them a hatred for the country; and the day may come when you will hear them saying, "This is the country that disfranchises us, and deprives us of our rights;" and you may see them coming back here from the United States with muskets in their hands.' I don't believe that in ten years from this time you will see a colored man in this country. We won't stay here after this war is decided; for I have my opinion in which way it is to be decided. I have told my children to stay in school until they are put out. 'If they tell you to go,' I have said to them, 'don't go, but wait until they lay hands on you to put you out; and then you come quietly home, and I will attend to it.' I have four children in the school, who go regularly, and are getting on very well; there is no complaint of them. I told the trustees if there was any complaint of their not behaving well, or any thing of the kind, to expel them from the school, or let me know."

This struggle between a fugitive slave and the school trustees of the city of London involves a great principle, and the decision of the Court will be looked for with interest, not only by the parties immediately concerned, but by multitudes in Canada. Nor should the interest be confined to that country; for the same question and the same struggle will arise in this.

Meantime, the question has been decided in favor of the right of the school trustees of London to establish a separate school for colored children by the highest authority short of the Court,—Dr. Ryerson, the Chief Superintendent of Public Instruction in Canada West. He said to us:—

"It is within the power of the school trustees in cities and towns to make a distinction between colors, for there they have the direction of all the schools; but in country places, where there are distinct school municipalities, it is at the option of the colored people to have separate schools or not. In some country places, the trustees have refused to admit colored children to the schools; the parents have appealed to me; I have referred them to the courts; and the courts have always given decisions in their favor."

It is conceded that the law authorizes the school trustees to establish separate schools for colored people upon their asking for them; it also authorizes school trustees in cities and towns to establish *separate* schools without such restriction. The obvious intent of giving this latter power was to meet the wants of Roman Catholics, who congregate in towns and cities. But notwithstanding this intent, the Chief Superintendent decides that, under the law, the trustees may establish separate schools for colored children, and exclude them from the schools for whites. This seems, to a layman, an extraordinary decision, however it may strike lawyers. It seems extraordinary, because the whole people, speaking through the laws, not only declared against distinctions which lead to the establishment of castes, but purposely ignored distinction of color among citizens. They established a government to carry out their will; and yet a subordinate branch of this government may use power derived from it to defeat that will, and to degrade part of the citizens on account of their color!

Moreover, it would seem that by permitting the School Trustees to establish separate schools upon the petition of colored people, the legislature did not contemplate the establishment of such schools *against* their will.

The spirit of the law clearly contemplated *common* schools, not compulsory *caste* schools; and if these can be established in virtue of any *by*-law, then verily, the letter killeth the spirit.

Underlying the great institution of the common school are two primal ideas, one of individual culture, the other of human brotherhood. In the common school house is held the first gathering of the Demos, in primary assemblage, never to be dissolved, only adjourned from day to day, through all time. The little people trained in the exercise of family love at home, come together in the school-house to enlarge the circle of their affections by loving other children of the greater human family, in its wider home—the world. Strange perversion, if the first moral lesson should be that of exclusion and caste!

It would be easy and agreeable to cite cases in which not only justice but good will is manifested towards the refugees. It is usually done in the towns where they make a very small proportion of the population. It is done in the University of Toronto, and in some other literary educational institutions. But upon the whole, there is a strong popular prejudice against the colored people, which operates greatly to the disadvantage of the refugees.

Then another disadvantage is to be considered. Emigrants going to a new country, especially to a cold one, need to make some preparation, and to take with them a little property. These refugees, however, could do neither. Those from the Slave States landed in Canada penniless, and without change of raiment. Those from the Free States brought small sums which they had earned; but very few had money enough for a month's subsistence. The Provincial Government did nothing for them; and the local authorities made no provision for employing them. Some money, indeed, has been raised by contribution in England and the United States, but most of this has been expended (with questionable wisdom) for establishing several communities, or agricultural colonies; for building up churches; and for supporting white agents in comfort. Very little of this money has been applied directly to the aid of the refugees.

Notwithstanding all these disadvantages, they have shown the will and the ability to work and to support themselves.

Disposition to Work.

No sensible people in Canada charge the refugees with slothfulness. The only charge worth notice is that they "shirk hard work." This charge is made thoughtlessly by most people; wrathfully by those who have to do the heavy drudgery. The gist of the matter, however, is this: In every civilized community there is a certain amount of hard work, requiring muscular effort, to be done by somebody. In Canada, as elsewhere, this work, instead of being made a blessing to all by fair and equal distribution, is made a grievous burden to one class, by being thrown exclusively on their shoulders, while another class suffers from lack of it.

Each white man tries to spare his own muscles, and to make some of his neighbors do his share of manual labor. If he must work, he prefers the lightest kind of labor. The negro stands by, and imitates the white man. Work he must; but, like his fugleman, he prefers the light kind; and he contrives to get it.

Men want to be shaved, and to have their boots blacked. They want also to have heavy hods carried up ladders; and wet mud shovelled out of ditches. There stand Irishmen, Germans, and negroes, seeking work. Each would prefer the lighter kind, especially as it is best paid. Each would prefer to exercise his fingers rather than his arms; and to wait and tend, rather than strain his back and weary his muscles. But the employer prefers the nimble-fingered negro for his light work, and the brawny-armed Irishman for his heavy work. So the negro shaves, and brushes, and tends, and frisks about; while his competitor delves, and swears that "a nigger is too lazy to work."

Sometimes the competition and contrast are very striking, as in hotels and boarding-houses. Here the colored men abound; but in these very houses, the porterage, and all heavy work and dirty work, are done by white men. If you ring your bell, the nimble mulatto who skips up to you in his white linen jacket, does not soil his dainty fingers by bringing the coal which you ask for, but sends a stalwart fireman, a traditionary white man, but so black and begrimed by coal, that in the South he might need free papers to prove his lineage.

In further proof of the mulatto's disposition to imitate the white man, and shift the heaviest burden to other men's shoulders, it may be stated that the colonists in Liberia do exactly as the exiles in Canada do, except that they use the native negroes, instead of Celts, to hew their wood and draw their water.

"I was astonished," says the Rev. Mr. Cowan, "to see in Harper, native women bringing up cord-wood on their heads from the landing on the river-bank to private dwellings, at twenty-five cents a day, while the colonist felt above such work."*

Verily, human nature does not change with time, nor does color affect it; for the old maxim may be applied to these colonists—"They who cross the sea change their sky, but not their spirit."

But mulattoes dislike hard manual labor, not only because it is held less respectable than light work or no work, but because by their very organization,—by their lymphatic temperament, and lack of animal vigor, they are less adapted to prolonged muscular effort than full breeds. That they do not lack industry and thrift, the condition of those in Canada proves clearly, for thousands and tens of thousands of colored people have there worked hard for a living, and have earned it.

First, there is negative proof of this, in the fact that they do not beg, and that they receive no more than their share of public support, if even so much. We traversed the whole length of Canada West three times, stopping at the places where colored people most abounded; going into their quarters in the cities, and visiting their farm-houses by the wayside; yet we met no beggars; and although there were evident signs of extreme poverty among those recently arrived, we did not see such marks of utter destitution and want, as may be found in the lower walks of life in most coun-

* "Liberia As I Found It." By Rev. A. Cowan, Agent of the Kentucky Colonization Society. p. 122.

tries. The following are fair specimens of the testimony given by intelligent white persons upon this point.

Hon. George Brown, M. P., of Toronto, says:—

"One thing about the colored people here is quite remarkable; they never beg. They only ask for work; and when they get work, if they have borrowed any money, they will come back and pay it — a thing I never knew white men to do. Their ministers are about the only beggars with black faces I have ever seen."

Mr. Park, a merchant of Malden, says:—

"Part of them (the colored population) are disposed to be industrious, and part of them are pretty indolent. They do n't take care of their own poor. We have no poor-house. The poor are relieved either by the government of the municipality, or by the people. The colored people get about the same assistance, in proportion to their numbers, that the whites do. I think they beg more than the whites do."

Mr. Brush, Town Clerk of Malden, says:—

"A portion of them (the colored people) are pretty well-behaved, and another portion not. We have a very small Irish laboring population. A great many of these colored people go and sail (are sailors) in the summer time, and in the winter, lie round, and do n't do much. The upper part of this town is inhabited by French people, the worst people in the world. There is not the toss of a copper between them and the colored people. We have to help a great many of them; more than any other class of people we have here. I have been Clerk of the Council for three years, and have had the opportunity of knowing. I think the Council have given more to the colored people than to any others."

In and about Malden the colored people congregate too numerously, and do not do so well as in other places.

The Rev. James Proudfoot, of London, says:—"I don't know a beggar among the colored people."

The great mass of the colored people of Canada have been thrown entirely upon their own resources; and their history is generally like that of a fugitive whom we met, who told us that on arrival, he had to borrow twenty-five cents to buy an axe, and from that day forward had worked on without asking favors, until he had become independent and comfortable.

There is a most striking contrast between these exiles,—penniless, unaided, in a cold climate, amid unsympathizing people,—and those who were sent, at great expense, across the ocean to an African climate, then supported entirely for six months, and afterwards aided and bolstered up by a powerful society, which still expend large sums for the support of the Colony. The first have succeeded; the latter have virtually failed. Let the lesson be pondered by those who are considering what shall be done with the negro.

But second, there is positive and tangible proof of the will and the ability of the colored people to work and support themselves, and gather substance even in the hard climate of Canada.

Property.

The Mayor of London says:—

"I think there are about seventy-five colored families here. They all pay taxes. They have not all got property, but every male over twenty-one pays the road tax of two dollars per annum. Some of them keep little huckster shops, but that is about as far as they go in that direction. There are none of any wealth, though there are a good many who own a single lot of land apiece."

Mr. William Clark, of London, says:—

"I don't know that there is any pauperism here among the colored people. They get work here, and some of them work very well indeed. I never knew of any difficulty with them here, any more than with white people. I have lived amongst them, and never had any difficulty with them at all. Some of them are very good, and some very bad — just like other people. They compare very favorably with the other laboring classes."

Col. Stephenson, of St. Catherines, says:—

"The negroes have furniture, whereas the Irish have none. Every copper of money the Irish get, they lay up; and the victuals they eat, they generally go out and beg from the people. I have seen an old woman here begging who had $1,700 in the bank. You could not get a negro to do that. We don't find many paupers among the negroes, as a general thing. There is one thing I have noticed; they cannot bear prosperity. If they get a little ahead, they won't work, unless they can get higher wages."

Dr. H. T. Ridley, of Hamilton, says:—

"I think the colored population are a very quiet, well-behaved set of people. My patients are able to pay a moderate fee. Full one-half of the colored people, I suppose, are able to pay nothing. I think they compare well with the lower Irish."

In another connection, he says:—

"Very few of the colored people beg. I do not know of a colored man who has come to me for a cent. They assist each other. There are a few who own lots in town, but there is no colored man here, that I know of, who is considered well off. I am one of the six physicians to the hospital, and I do not think the colored people send any greater proportion there than the whites."

The town records of Malden, show that there are in all 550 tax-payers in that town, of whom 71 are colored. The annual value of the property on which they were assessed, in 1863, was $1,253, on which a tax of 29 per cent. was levied, — amounting to $363.37 — or about $5.12 to each tax-payer. The total tax of the town was $4,916.37; leaving $4,553.00 to be paid by the whites — or an average of $9.52 to each. Assuming the population given by Mr. Brush to be correct, there is one white tax-payer to three and one-third of the white inhabitants, and one colored tax-payer to every eleven of the colored inhabitants.

By the books of the assessors of Chatham, it appears that the total number of rate-payers in the town for the year 1863 was 1,021, of whom 134 were colored. The total amount of tax collected was $10,179.79; of which the 134 colored rate-payers contributed $667.45 — or $4.98 apiece, on an average. The 887 white rate-payers contributed $9,433.34—or $10.63 apiece. The total population of Chatham is given at 4,466, and the colored population estimated at 1,300. It thus appears that the white tax-payers are about one to every three and a half of the white population, and the colored about one to every thirteen of the colored population.

By the books of the town clerk of Windsor, it appears that there are 152 colored tax-payers in the town, and 448 white. The total annual value of the property for which the colored people are taxed amounts to $2,648 —affording a tax of $635.52; which, deducted from the total tax, ($9,000,) leaves $8,364.48 to be paid by the whites. Taking the colored population at 750, this shows one tax-payer to every *five* of the population; and estimating the white population at 3,250, there is one white tax-payer to every seven and one-fourth of the white population. The average amount paid by each colored tax-payer is $4.18; by each white tax-payer, $18.76.

In Toronto, a city of 44,821 inhabitants, of whom about 900 are colored, the books of the tax collectors show the following amount paid by colored persons:—

St. John's ward, $665.24; St. Andrew's ward, $549.55; St. Lawrence's ward, $388; St. David's ward, $37.25; St. Patrick's ward, $347.63; St. George's ward, $75.95; St. James's ward, $261.57. Total, $2,345.19.

In addition to this, an income tax is assessed on all colored persons earning over $200 a year.

We found that only fifteen colored persons deposited money in the Savings Banks, averaging $15 each. They have use for all their means, and do not hoard.

But the surest sign of their thrift is the appearance of their dwelling-houses, farms, stock, tools and the like. In these, moreover, we find encouraging signs for the negros, because they show that he feels so strongly the family instinct, and the desire to possess land and a dwelling-place.

They were badly advised when they settled in suburbs by themselves; and the wiser ones now see that it would be better for them, as it doubtless would for the whole community, to have their dwellings scattered among those of the whites, as they are in Hamilton and Toronto, rather than to live in separate quarters, as they do in St. Catherines, Chatham, and other places.

But whether scattered about, or collected in suburbs, the dwellings of the refugees are generally superior to those of the Irish, or other foreign emigrants of the laboring class. Most certainly they are far superior to the negro huts upon slave plantations, which many of them formerly inhabited. Indeed, in point of neatness of premises, they are superior to the dwellings of the "poor whites," and even of small planters; a doubtful compliment, for those not only lack out-buildings, but are usually dirty and comfortless. The refugees for the most part live in small, tidy houses; not shanties, with old hats sticking out of broken windows. Their habitations are not filthy huts, in filthy grounds, but comfortable dwellings, in good repair. Many are owned by the occupants. They have little gardens, which seem well cared for. This is the case not only in the Colonies, as they are called, where the form and dimensions of the houses are prescribed by the Company, but in those places where the refugees are entirely free to live as they choose. In the outskirts of Chatham and other large places are scores of small two-story houses, with garden lots, owned and inhabited by refugees who came to the country penniless.

We visited many of these houses, and found that the decencies of life are well observed, and that the comforts of life are not wanting. Cooking, eating, and sleeping, are not done in the same room, but in separate ones. They are tidily furnished; and some have carpets on the floors; and curtains at the windows. It is pleasant to see the feeble dawnings of taste in rude pictures, and simple attempts at ornament.

Their tables are decently spread, and plentifully supplied. It is evident that they spend more money upon their households than foreign emigrants do. They live better; and they clothe their children better. They say, indeed, that this is the reason they do not lay up so much money as many Irish and Germans do.

Says Mrs. Brown, (colored,) of St. Catherines:—

"I have been here fifteen years, and we have paid taxes all the time. A good many of the colored people own their own houses, and have owned them ever since I came here. When they came here, of course they were destitute and had nothing. Most of them came from the Slave States. There are some here who are doing very well. The reason they do not get so much property as the Irish is because the Irish will live on little, or nothing. They live like pigs, and worse than pigs. The colored people can't live, like the Irish, on potatoes and salt. They want something to eat, if they have to work. An Irishman will take potatoes and salt, and a sup of milk, and say nothing about it; but as a people, we are used to living different from that, and can't do it."

There are exceptions, of course; and some families, especially new comers, live crowded up in one room. They cannot do otherwise at first; but as soon as they have secured the necessaries of life, they begin to imitate the older settlers, and to look for its comforts, and then for some of its luxuries. As a general thing, the condition of the house, the abundance of furniture, and the presence of ornament, denote the time which the refugee has enjoyed freedom. A family arrives to-day, without a rag of clothing, except what they wear; and without a cent of money. Of course, they must huddle into one room; and by a little help from their fellows, feed and warm themselves as they best can. In ten years, that same family will probably inhabit a decent house, with tidy furniture, and a plentiful table. Such has been the history of hundreds and thousands of Canadian refugees.

It is difficult to collect any reliable statistics of the property of the colored people in the rural districts. They are widely scattered, and the tax-rolls do not distinguish them from whites. It is certain, however, that they are generally thriving; and it is probable that they are doing even better than those who are more closely congregated. Some have small gardens near large towns, which they help to supply with vegetables. On all market days, they are seen going into town with their carts, laden with garden stuffs; the man generally accompanied by his wife or children; often both, so social are they. They form an industrious and useful class.

Another class is formed by the small farmers, who are more widely scattered. Little is heard about them, except when the prejudice of the Irish, or other rude people, is roused to passion by some competition of interest, or personal collision, and then there is a talk about the "nuisance of niggers."

They generally own the land which they occupy; and in many cases they have paid off the mortgages, and hold a clear fee. Indeed, one of the most hopeful signs is the general desire to own land, and work for themselves.

Now and then is seen the miserable cabin of a negro squatter, who evidently sleeps by day, and prowls by night. This, however, is the exception. As a general rule, the farms of negroes, although inferior to the first-class farms of their region in point of cultivation, fences, stock, and the like, are quite equal to the average of second-class farms. So the colored farmers, though not equal to the first-class white farmers, compare very well with the average of the second-class. They have not the capital, nor the intelligence, nor the skill of the best farmers. But they are not lazy, nor stupid, nor thriftless; on the contrary, they keep their lands and premises in tolerable condition; and they support themselves without recourse to public charity. Such men are valuable members of any agricultural community. If not the best, they are far from being the worst.

We rode through some of the rural districts, and stopped at many farm houses. The most remarkable thing is that the farm houses of colored people are seldom to be distinguished from those of whites by the external appearance. There is no special look of poverty or slovenliness about them. You have to watch for the appearance of some person in order to know, by his color, whether it is the house of whites, or not.

Usually, the condition of the land and premises about the house, indicates the length of time which the refugee has occupied them. Those who have come from the United States within a year or two, live in a log cabin, in a small cleared lot; around which is the forest or wild land. Older settlers have built houses, and cleared larger fields; and they keep a cow, a pig, and some poultry. A few have well-cleared farms and good outbuildings, with plenty of farm tools, horses, oxen, cows, and the like.

The following notes, made on a day's journey through a rural district, will give some idea of the people whom we met upon the road:—

"Tuesday, September 15, left Amherstburg for Colchester. Before passing out of the township of Malden, in which Amherstburg is situated, stopped at the farm of Mr. Buckner—a colored man. The place is under good cultivation; has a number of fine cattle upon it; and every thing about indicates thrift and care. Further on, called at a log cabin occupied by a colored family, who had rented the place. The women only were at home, who said they were getting along very well with the farm. The younger of the two women was uncommonly bright and intelligent, and both of them kind and civil-spoken. At another house, saw an old lady, who said she was from Kentucky, where she had been free, but her husband was a slave. She said she had worked harder in Canada, trying to get a start, than she ever did in Kentucky. She thought the climate not so healthy as that of Kentucky, especially for children, who took colds, and were somehow carried off, she said, very fast. She declared that she would go back to the old home when freedom was established in the States.

Later, stopped at a wayside tavern, kept by French people. The woman said the colored people were good neighbors, except that they would pilfer small things. Met a man on horseback, who said the blacks were poor farmers, and did not do so well as the most inferior class of whites. They did not know any thing about farming, he said, and when hired, required to be told every fifteen minutes what to do and how to do it. He thought the climate prejudicial to children. The "darkies," he said, were charged with stealing a good deal, but he thought they did n't steal any more than some white people. He thought the thefts of white men were often charged upon the blacks.

Stopped at another tavern, kept by a Frenchman, who said the blacks were good-natured, and not disposed to be quarrelsome, but given to pilfering. When asked if they were any worse in that respect than the whites, he said perhaps they were, a little, but it was hard to say which were the worse. Here were two fugitives from Kentucky. One of them said he had been in the place six years, and worked out as a laborer, getting 50 cents a day for common work, 62½ cents for cutting corn, and $1 a day for harvesting, and found. He said he could not lay by any thing, having a wife and three children to support. He was anxious to have a place of his own, he said, but had no means to buy one. His children did not go to school at all, for there was no school for colored children, and the whites would not permit his children to go to their school.

Saw a little cabin near the road, and a colored man and woman, and some children about. On being interrogated, the man said he was from North Carolina, and "allowed" he found Canada a hard place to get a living in. He would be glad, he said, to get back to the States, as soon as he could be free there. The woman said she was from Virginia, and that the prejudice was "a heap" stronger in Canada than it was at home. The people, she said, seemed to think the blacks "wern't folks, any way." She was anxious to go back.

Met a farmer, who said the blacks were the worst people round. They wern't good for any thing, unless a man wanted them to work, and then, if they were looked after "right sharp," they would do pretty well. He did n't know that the blacks stole any more than the whites, but thought the whites often got clear by saddling their sins on the backs of the "darkies."

Returning, visited and inspected the colored school at Amherstburg. Number of scholars on the roll, 90; average attendance, 60."

Colonies.

There is another class of colored people to whom no reference has yet been made, and they are called the "Colonists."

The refugees have always received from the government of Canada welcome and protection; from the better class of people, goodwill and justice; and from a few, active friendship and important assistance. These friends, with other benevolent persons in the United States and Great Britain, have, at various periods, got up organizations for the relief and the aid of the refugees. These organizations have generally taken the form of societies for procuring tracts of land, and building up communities of colored people, called colonies.

The principal of these are the Elgin settlement, at Buxton, the Dawn settlement, at Dresden, and the Refugees' Home, near Windsor.

It is evident that the attempts of organized societies to settle the colored people in colonies, by themselves, are of less interest to the people of the United States, than are the attempts of refugees to maintain themselves, without any aid.

It is unknown how much assistance the Colonists receive from the money power of societies and the moral power of the agents. It is indeed ungracious to criticise, where the efforts have been so generous and the success so satisfactory; but there are various objections to the plans and proceedings of the colonizing societies. The negroes, going into an inhabited and civilized country, should not be systematically congregated in communities. Their natural affinities are strong enough to keep up all desirable relations without artificial encouragement. Experience shows that they do best when scattered about, and forming a small proportion of the whole community.

Next, the discipline of the colonies, though it only subjects the negroes to what is considered useful apprenticeship, does prolong a dependence which amounts almost to servitude; and does not convert them so surely into hardy, self-reliant men, as the rude struggle with actual difficulties, which they themselves have to face and to overcome, instead of doing so through an agent.

Taken as a whole, the colonists have cost to somebody a great deal of money, and a great deal of effort; and they have not succeeded so well as many who have been thrown entirely upon their own resources.

While commending to careful attention the accounts given by Mr. King of the colony at Buxton, it is just to say that some intelligent persons, friends of the colored people, and familiar with their condition, believe that in none of the colonies, not even in Buxton, do they succeed so well, upon the whole, as those who are thrown entirely upon their own resources.

Nevertheless, these colonies are worthy of more attention than we were able to give them.

We visited Buxton, and received from Mr. King, its founder and father, an account of its history and condition, which will be found, in a condensed form, in the Appendix. He reports, and evidently believes fully, that the colony has been a perfect success.

Be this as it may, Buxton is certainly a very interesting place. Sixteen years ago, it was a wilderness. Now, good highways are laid out in all directions through the forest; and by their side, standing back thirty-three feet from the road, are about two hundred cottages, all built on the same pattern, all looking neat and comfortable. Around each one is a cleared space, of several acres, which is well cultivated. The fences are in good order; the barns seem well filled; and cattle, and horses, and pigs, and poultry, abound. There are signs of industry, and thrift, and comfort, every where; signs of intemperance, of idleness, of want, nowhere. There is no tavern, and no groggery; but there is a chapel and school-house.

Most interesting of all are the inhabitants. Twenty

years ago, most of them were slaves, who owned nothing, not even their children. Now they own themselves; they own their houses and farms; and they have their wives and children about them. They are enfranchised citizens of a government which protects their rights. They have the great essentials for human happiness, "something to love, something to do, and something to hope for;" and if they are not happy, it is their own fault.

The present condition of all these colonists, as compared with their former one, is very remarkable; but no limner could desire a stronger contrast for two pictures of life than the history of one of them presents. Seventeen years ago, he was a chattel; a thing to be worked and flogged, bought and sold, like a horse. He inhabited a wretched hut, with a woman who could not be his lawful wife, and with dirty children, begotten by them, but owned by another, and whom they were rearing until large enough for the owner to work or to sell. Sad as was his actual condition, there was nothing to be hoped for in the future; and every thing to be feared.

At last, in desperation, he stole away by night from his master's plantation in Missouri; and stole, besides himself, something for food and covering, which he bore on his back; and also his little boy, whom he carried in his arms. He stole also the woman, and the other children, who followed him, trembling with fear and cold, through the darkness, and towards the north star. Sad procession! but only one of the many which have been continually moving, by night, from the house of bondage, towards the land of freedom.

The flight was long, and painful, and dangerous. Then followed years of toil, and poverty, and anxiety. Then came, little by little, success, and comfort, and hope. And now, the scene had quite changed; and we found that man standing erect and bold, upon his own well-tilled farm, in front of his own house, into which he politely invited us. The woman had become his lawful wife, the proud mistress of a tidy household. The dirty toddling chattels had grown to be comely youth and maidens; and the little boy whom he bore away in his arms, was a fine, manly fellow, a student at Knox College, but now spending his vacation *at home.*

The man took a natural pride in his prosperity; and dilated upon the fertility of his acres, the excellence of his stock, and the fleetness of his horses.

When the pressing invitation to stay and partake his hospitality was declined, on the ground of lack of time, he said, with pardonable vanity, "I can send you in a wagon of *my own*, and behind a pair of my own horses, who will take you to Chatham, in less time than you can get there with your team."

Some of the refugees are

Mechanics.

There are plasterers and white-washers in all the large towns; and there are also a few excellent blacksmiths, and some tolerable carpenters. We found one man running a windmill, which he had constructed with his own hands; and which, though very shaky in appearance, furnished good power.

A colored man is said by many to be the best gunsmith in Canada West. He certainly makes beautiful pistols.

The most interesting sight in the way of mechanical industry was in Hamilton, where a young man named Hill had established himself. He is a fine, athletic young man, who must have come of good stock, for, said he, "The whole of our family bought ourselves."

"I came away from Virginia," continued he, "because I didn't like the condition of things there. I didn't like to be trod upon. A colored man there, let him be free born or not, must carry a scrap of paper in his pocket to show that he is free, or he cannot move. He is not really free, because if he wants to go to New York, for instance, he must get a white man to vouch for his freedom.

"We are manufacturers of tobacco, and there are merchants here who have agreed to take all we can manufacture, and to encourage us all they possibly can. I came from the South in September, 1853, and my family followed in December. My wife had to get a voucher for her freedom, before she could come on. Sometimes they put obstructions in the way of free people coming away, if they are so disposed. I was in slavery until I was about eighteen years old. There were four uncles, myself and mother, and another sister of my uncles. My uncles paid fifteen hundred dollars apiece for themselves. They bought themselves three times. They got cheated out of their freedom in the first two instances, and were put in jail at one time, and were going to be sold down South, right away; but parties who were well acquainted with us, and knew we had made desperate struggles for our freedom, came forward and advanced the money, and took us out of jail, and put us on a footing so that we could go ahead and earn money to pay the debt. We have an uncle in Pittsburg, who has accumulated a good deal of property since he obtained his freedom. My uncles bought me and my mother, as well as themselves. I saw a great deal of slavery; and not only that, but my parents had to undergo a great deal of hardship in their earlier days. I never suffered any particular hardship myself. I had a grandfather who had long been free, and when the boys grew up, he would take them and learn them a trade, and keep them out of the hands of the traders; and when they became men and women, having had his industry instilled into them, they would be able and willing to work."

We found Mr. Hill, and his three colored partners in business, working very earnestly and vigorously, with brawny arms, in a tobacco manufactory of their own. They had recently hired a building at two hundred and fifty dollars a year; made most of the wood-work of their machinery themselves, and started their business. By diligent and faithful work, they soon drew custom, and their prospect seemed excellent. They employed about twenty hands, among whom were three white boys; for, said Hill, "hands are scarce, you see, and we have to take *any we can get.* We are adding to our numbers, and as soon as all the machinery is going, we expect to have fifty workmen."

The sight of this establishment would astonish those who think negroes too stupid for business, and too lazy for work. It was planned and carried on by colored people, with money of their own earning. It was marked by the order, silence, and earnestness which pervade all good workshops. There was no talking, laughing, or looking about. Every man was busy at his task. Some were heaving down the press with ponderous iron levers; some were filling boxes; others nailing them up; some assorting the stock, and others rolling it into plugs. Each seemed to have the kind of work best suited to him; the men using their brawny arms for lifting and pulling; the boys their tiny fingers for picking and sorting. They were paid in proportion to the worth of their work; and each worked "with a will."

"We mean to succeed," said Hill, "and we think we shall; for we understand the business, and mean to do better work than others do; and merchants will find that out fast enough." The calm assurance with which he spoke, would have secured good names on the back of his note, if he had been unwise enough to ask credit.

The history of this family shows the effect of culture upon good stock. Not all the depressing and demoralizing influences of a slave community could repress their energy or prevent their success.

Another class is that of

Sailors.

The good will of "old salts" to negroes is proverbial. In the old merchant packet, the steward was usually a colored man; and so was the cook, who was always dubbed "doctor." His "caboose" was a favorite resort in dog-watch; and he was the life of the forecastle. The principal objection to shipping a colored man was, that he was apt to charm some Desdemona, who would insist upon marrying him and keeping him in England; leaving the ship to make the homeward passage minus steward, or "doctor;" unless, perchance, some former victim had become disenchanted, and inclined to fly to America for freedom.

Even now, in the navy, your "true blue" will mess with the negro, and rather likes his company. The fresh-water sailors on the lakes and rivers seem to share the liberality of "blue-water salts," and not to object to "colored company," unless, indeed, there is too much of it.

It is curious to observe how here, as elsewhere, the individual negro awakens sympathy as a fellow man; that one, in a "mess," is a boon companion; but that two or three, excite antagonism and awaken prejudice. The root of the evil is not in any natural antipathy, but that "business" is conducted in the spirit of antagonism instead of co-operation.

There are many of the refugees who "go down to the *lakes* in ships, that do business on the great waters;" and these fresh-water sailors earn good wages in summer.

No opportunity presented of seeing this class, but the general report about them was, that they "loafed round in winter, and spent all their earnings." This is proof that they do work and earn money; and if they spend it just as other tars do, the fact only proves that the vocation of sailor affects blacks as it does whites.

Captain Averill, of Malden, says:—

"Colored men do very well for deck hands, and firemen, and the like of that. They are the best men we have. We have to pay them the same as white men, and I prefer them to some portion of our citizens. We have to keep them separate from white sailors. We cannot mix them. We always either carry a black crew or a white one. We will take a crew of firemen, darkies, or a crew of deck hands, darkies. They are fully as good as white sailors, in regard to temperance. We can put more confidence in them than we can in white men. The colored men are not much inclined to lay up their wages. They spend their money just about as fast as they go along. Some of them will stay about a boat all summer long, and not take up any wages of consequence; and when you can get a man like that he is very valuable, because he will influence the others. They don't get to places of confidence. We never make them mates. None of them own any crafts."

More evidence might be cited; but enough has been

given to show that with freedom, and the ordinary motives for industry, the colored people will be diligent and thrifty.

It is plain, however, that upon the whole, the physical organization of a mixed breed like this one, does not adapt men to hard and continuous muscular labor; and that they will naturally seek and find in the industrious ranks of society, certain places not requiring such labor, which they can fill profitably to the community and to themselves.

Section 4.

Intellectual and Moral Condition.

An unusually large proportion of the colored population of Canada is made up of adults. Those from the Free States had very little schooling in youth; those from the Slave States, none at all. Considering these things, it is rather remarkable that so many can now read and write. Moreover, they show their esteem for instruction by their desire to obtain it for their children. They all wish to have their children go to school, and they send them all the time that they can be spared.

Canada West has adopted a good system of public instruction, which is well administered. The common schools, though inferior to those of several of the States of the United States, are good. Colored children are admitted to them in most places; and where a separate school is opened for them, it is as well provided by government with teachers and apparatus as the other schools are. Notwithstanding the growing prejudice against blacks, the authorities evidently mean to deal justly by them in regard to instruction; and even those who advocate separate schools, promise that they shall be equal to white schools.

We had no adequate means of ascertaining exactly how many colored scholars there are in proportion to the whole population; but conclude, from what data could be had, that it is almost as large as the proportion of white scholars to the white population. In Chatham, for instance, there is one white scholar to 11½ of the white population; and one colored scholar to 12 of the colored population. The average daily attendance of scholars in the colored schools is seventy per cent.; the average attendance in the white schools is a fraction over seventy. Now, in Chatham, the colored people are quite as unfavorably situated as in any other places; and considering that they are all of the industrious class, who need the services of their children, the number of scholars they send, and their average of daily attendance, are high. It is generally stated, however, that the black children do not attend school so many years as the white do; and this is doubtless for the reason above assigned, that their parents more generally have need of their services at home.

The colored children, in the mixed schools, do not differ in their general appearance and behavior from their white comrades. They are usually clean and decently clad. They look quite as bright as the whites; and are perhaps a little more mirthful and roguish. The association is manifestly beneficial to the colored children. Says Mr. McCullum, principal of the high school at Hamilton,—

"I am impressed with the idea that colored persons brought up among whites look better than others; their rougher, harsher features disappear. I think that colored children, brought up among white people, look better than their parents."

The appearance, and the acquirements of colored children in the separate schools, are less satisfactory They do not look so tidy; and are not so well ordered as children of the same class in the white schools. Moreover, they are more backward in their studies.

The colored people were unwise in asking for separate schools at all; and those who asked for colored teachers made a further mistake; because the chance of getting a good one was small, the range of selection being very limited. Had they merely required *good* teachers, irrespective of color, they would have had more men like Mr. Sinclair, to elevate, as well as teach their children.

They must, in justice to the whites, acknowledge that in the matter of separate schools and of separate churches, they themselves have yielded to the natural affinities of race which lie at the root of those very prejudices about which they complain so much. They must acknowledge, moreover, that the authorities endeavor to provide as good instruction for their children as for white children.

With regard to the comparative mental capacity of colored and white children, teachers differ in opinion. Dr. McCaul, president of the university at Toronto, bears very strong testimony in favor of the first. He says:—

"I can give you my own experience in regard to the capacity of the blacks. There was a boy here from Upper Canada by the name of Galigo, who, I think I am safe in saying, was a thorough black. He did exceedingly well, and manifested a capacity equal to any white boy of his standing. We had a mulatto here this last examination, who took the 'double-first' in both classics and mathematics. He has very great ability. There are very few whites who can do what he did. It would be considered a rare thing to have a 'double-first' got once in five years, and that amongst the highest 'honor-men.' The 'honor-men,' as we call them, are in the ratio of one to thirty. There was very great competition, but he carried off the prize. He expected to come out first of all in mathematics, but he failed in that; but he came out in the first class of honors, in both classics and mathematics, as no one else in the year did; and I do not think there have been more than three instances in which it has been done since the university was opened, twenty years ago. Laferty is the young man's name. His father was a man of very humble capacity, and, I think, a full black. There was another man who was a student here, who did very well in medicine—Dr. Augusta. There was another medical student here,—Mr. Abbott,—who got along very well. I do not hesitate at all to say, with regard to Mr. Laferty, that he is fully equal to any white man, and, as I mentioned to you, far superior to the average of them. It was a great subject of astonishment to some of our Kentucky friends, who came over here last year in October, when they saw this mulatto get the first prize for Greek verse, which he had to recite; and he was the crack man of the day, all the others listening to him with great pleasure."

Mr. McCullum, of Hamilton, says:—

"I have spoken to the teachers at the school, in reference to the colored pupils, and they all coincide in the opinion I have given, that they are fully equal to the others, in mental attainments, and in their conduct and discipline at school."

Mr. Sinclair, principal of the school at Chatham, says:—

"On the whole, I think the colored children learn about the same as whites. The only difference I have observed is this—

that in one week they learn faster than the whites ; but then, they require frequent reviews, so that, on the whole, it is about the same."

This is the testimony of enlightened men, who have given attention to the matter ; but they are men of liberal and generous natures, whose sympathies are with the colored people, because of their need of them. Other teachers think less favorably of the mental capacity of colored children.

But, however it may be in schools, and in regard to the power of acquiring knowledge, the theory of the mental equality of colored and white people does not seem to be confirmed by the condition of the refugees in Canada. Some of them have been there a long time ; and a young generation is growing up. They do not lack ambition ; and yet they do not rise to stations requiring mental vigor. Great allowance, indeed, is to be made for the bitter prejudice against them, and for other disadvantages. But on the other hand, it is to be considered that when they are dispersed among the whites, the prejudice is not called out. And then it must be admitted, that among people of culture, there is a disposition to give them fair play. Nay, such people would probably regard a young man of real force of character with favor, on account of his being colored ; and would help him on. Two or three of this kind have been so treated ; but all must admit that the number of superior young men who have appeared is very small indeed.

The colored people of Canada, like those of the Free States, have sharp eyes and ears. They are quick of preception ; very imitative ; and they rapidly become intelligent. But they are rather knowing, than thinking people. They occupy useful stations in life; but such as require quick perceptions, rather than strong sense.

We have not the data for the final solution of the question of mental equality. Time alone can supply them. Not only must all the depressing influences of slavery be removed from one generation, but there must be several generations of free men; of men free from the consequences of slavery, and free from social ostracism, before that question can be determined. But, admitting that the colored breed has physical vitality enough to persist and to maintain itself in the competition of coming generations for subsistence, it is not certain that its members will have moral force enough to recover from the depression which so long existence as social pariahs has produced. Be this as it may, we have now, for the solution of the question, only limited observation and *a priori inferences.* These seem to point to the mental inferiority of the half breeds, if not of the negroes.

An opinion is held by some teachers of colored schools in the Northern States, that their scholars advance as fast as whites in all the elementary studies, but fail when they come to studies which tax the higher mental powers, or the reasoning and combining faculties. That is, that the perceptive faculties, which take cognizance of things, and of their names and qualities, are as keen in the blacks as in the whites; but that the reasoning faculties, which generalise from the knowledge gathered by the perceptive faculties, are not.

This is probably true with regard to pure blacks, if not to mulattoes also. Now, the perceptive faculties are nearly allied to the instincts, which men share equally with other animals; while the reasoning and reflecting faculties are superior to them, and are midway between that animal nature common to men and brutes which holds us down to the earth with them, and those higher qualities, or peculiarly human attributes, which lift us towards heaven. Superior activity of the lower or perceptive faculties may arise from greater development of that part of the animal organization which keeps us in relation with the organisms next below us in the scale of creation.

But this question of mental equality between pure blacks and whites is an ethnological one—a question about races; while we have only to do with a breed,—that of mulattoes. This breed in its mental organization seems to be partially emasculated. It has less of the elements out of which grow ferocity, but also less of energy and virilty, than pure blacks or whites.

Mulattoes seem to be, among races, what eunuchs are among individual men. They have less animalization than blacks, and less spiritualization than whites.

In concluding this part of the subject, a statement may be made, which, standing alone, is worth nothing; but which, if supported by wider observation, may be of some value. The colored persons met with in Canada, who had most force of character, were either nearly negroes, or nearly whites; that is, they bore strongly marked characteristics of one or the other race; not merely in the color of the skin, but in the character of other parts of their organization.

Moral Condition—Criminal Statistics.

It is difficult to convey a correct idea of the mental status of the refugees; but still more to give satisfactory evidence concerning their moral condition. Bare statistics are worth little. School returns have to be taken with great allowance; prison returns with still greater. With proper allowances, criminal statistics are worth something.

The Provincial Penitentiary at Kingston has been established twenty-seven years; during which time 375 colored persons have been committed, for the following offences:—

Arson, 5; murder, 9; rape, or assault with intent, 14; felony, 127; larceny, 220. Of these, 286 were born in the United States; 81 in British America; and 8 in the West Indies.

At the time of committal, fifty-seven of the convicts were between 10 and 20 years of age; one hundred and seventy were between 20 and 30; ninety-one were between 30 and 40; thirty-six were between 40 and 50; sixteen were between 50 and 60; and five were between 60 and 70.

Dr. Litchfield, the very obliging Superintendent of the Asylum for Criminal Lunatics, connected with the Penitentiary, says:—

"I cannot draw any reliable inference from the records, in respect to the comparative criminality of the white, red, or black man; because the census returns in regard to the African and Indian races, in the Province, at the time the last census was taken, are so manifestly wrong, that no correct calculation can be based upon them."

There are, at this time, 64 colored convicts in the Penitentiary. Taking the colored population as set down in the census of 1860, this gives one convict to every 191 inhabitants. But estimating the colored people at 15,000, (and this is a very low estimate,) it gives only one in 234⅜.

With regard to the conduct of the colored convicts, Dr. Litchfield says:—

> "The negro, as met with in Canada, is uniformly docile, courteous, kindly, and submissive; and he exhibits these qualities in a marked degree, in the Penitentiary."

This is corroborated by the County Jailers, who generally say that colored prisoners are more docile than white.

Statistics of minor offences, collected from the jail returns, will be found in the Appendix.

Any inferences from them as to the moral status of the colored people should be made with due allowance for the fact that a large portion of them arrived in Canada utterly destitute, and also for the significant fact stated in the testimony of the Hon. George Brown, M. P. Said he:—

> "I regard the colored people of Canada as a useful class of citizens. All their vices grow out of their former condition of slavery. Thieving is natural to them. But one thing you must bear in mind; *it will not do to trust the criminal statistics, for if a man with a black face is put into the box*, it is almost tantamount to conviction."

It will be seen that the most common offences of which the colored people are convicted are not those of violence, implying ferocity and passion,—not crimes against the person, but against property.

In public opinion, they lack that form of honesty which those who consider money as the chief end of man, regard as highest in the scale of virtues. It is curious to observe how vehemently the refugees are denounced in Canada, as the slaves are in the United States, for their utter insensibility to the right of property. Religious people, north and south, marvel that even converted and pious slaves do not abstain from picking and stealing; as if those who never in their lives knew anything of *meum*, should suddenly know all about *tuum*.

We boast of our white national virtues, and acknowledge that they grow out of freedom, but forget that the vices of slaves grow out of slavery; or, as has been better said—"The customs of a free people are part of their freedom; those of an enslaved people are part of their slavery."* Men going from slavery to freedom cannot change their habits as they change their garments. And it is to be remembered that the offences against property, with which by public voice the refugees are charged, are those so common in the south, and which grow directly out of slavery.

Respect of property is grafted by civilization upon natural morality. It needs culture, and is of slow growth. The lowest savages respect no kinds of property; and the highest but few. Now, the supposed interest of the slaveholder has been to keep the negroes as near the savage state as is consistent with the profitable culture of

* Les coutumes d'un peuple esclave sont une partie de leur esclavage; celles d'un peuple libre sont une partie de leur libertè.—*Montesquieu, Esprit des Lois, Liv. XIX. Chap.* 27.

cotton and sugar. He wants the negro not to steal, forgetting that a man must own something in order to have any adequate conception of what theft means.

The immorality of theft, however, has its degrees; and these seem to depend upon the natural right of ownership, rather than upon the conventional or legal right. The right of a man to his life and freedom, and to his young children, are manifest and indisputable, for they depend not upon human laws. No man can be intelligent enough to cultivate cotton, without feeling this instinctively, whether he forms a clear conception of it or not. He must feel, too, that the rights of property grow less sacred as they affect the owner less closely—as right in clothes, wares, horses, dogs, and the like; until they become very doubtful in fish and game, and things *feræ natura.* The owner, in his daily practice, violates the most sacred right of property, by taking the slave's labor without pay; and the slave imitates him by violating the less sacred right of property, in stealing what he can lay his hands on. The fact that there is any honesty at all left among them is proof of the natural strength of their moral nature.

The slaves come to Canada with these habits, which seem to have been made a part of their very nature by generations of servitude; and yet they rapidly lay them aside. Being free from the debasing influences of fear, and in the midst of a community where the rights of property are ranked among the most sacred things, as soon as they earn anything honestly, they feel the pride of ownership, and learn to respect the rights of others.

Religion.

It has been well said, that the slaveholders used the very virtues of the negroes to hold them in slavery. The master, like the devil, knew how to quote scripture for wicked purposes; and moulded the religious belief of the negroes into such form that he could appeal to it to compass his own ends, in violation of the spirit of true religion.

It is among the proofs of the strong religious nature of the negroes, that their faith endures shocks which would upset that of ordinary men. Slaves of pious, prayerful masters, have grown to manhood in the firm belief that it would be a sin against Heaven to leave the service of a master who exacts life-long toil without reward, and who would sell one of their children as he would sell a cow or a pig, when he wanted cash.

A touching instance of the struggle between what he believed to be a religious obligation to serve his mistress and a natural longing for freedom, is to be found in the narrative of Thomas Johnson, a Canadian refugee. He was so intelligent and faithful, that he was entrusted with the management of the farm. He came to the conclusion that he had a right to free his wife and three youngest children, and therefore got them off to Canada. He, himself, remained more than a year, and performed what he believed to be his duty to his mistress. Her friends, however, having an eye to their own future property, feared that if she should die, the slave would prefer to go and work for his own wife and children, rather than for them, and so they persuaded her to convert him into cash. Finding he was to be sold, "down south," he escaped across the river into Ohio. But his conscience troubled him. He could not bear the thought that he, who had been trusted on account of his honesty, should become a *mean runaway;* and he sent word that if instead of being "sent south," he could be sold to a certain man in the neighborhood, whom he thought to be humane, he would go back and finish his earthly pilgrimage in bondage. While waiting for the reply, he thought he would visit his wife and children, and take a last farewell; but when he found himself in Canada and really a free man, the natural bonds of affection proved stronger than those of a perverted religious sense, and kept him there, to discharge his duties to himself and his family.*

There are many touching instances of slaves who had borne good religious and moral characters, when forced by some gross outrage to run away, throwing themselves on the ground, and bemoaning their downfall, as they supposed—"I, an elder,—I, whom master and everybody trusted,—I to become a mean runaway!" &c.

Churches, &c.

Whenever a few refugees congregate together, the first thing they do in common is to provide for public worship. They have a passion for a church. Not merely a church spiritual, but a church material; and it must be good-looking, too. Wherever there are a few families gathered together, they get up a meeting-house of some kind. When they increase in numbers, they split up into various sects, and each sect must have a meeting-house of its own. They do not wait for the first one to

* Drew, pp. 379, 380, 381.

become full; for none of them do become full, because the people subdivide, and swarm off. They expend an undue and unreasonable part of their time and substance in building churches; and their zeal leads them to go begging for aid in the work. Their ministers have canvassed the United States and England, contribution box in hand; and by appealing to sectarian zeal, got the means of building up tabernacles of brick or wood, trusting to their own zeal for gathering a congregation. All this shows that the religious nature of these people, being but imperfectly developed, needs to be exhibited in the concrete form.

They improve, however, in this respect, under freedom, and manifest their religious instinct under higher forms than slaves do. It is a common remark that the religion of the negroes in slavery is purely emotional; that it does not prevent sinful lives; and that the most pious of them lie and steal without hesitation and without remorse. A little reflection will show that it could not well be otherwise. The religious instinct is certainly very strong in the negro, and it must have gratification in some outward manifestation; either in the lowest form of adoration of God, to secure personal preference with Him, here and hereafter; or in duty to God, shown by obeying the natural laws of conscience and morality as His laws; or in love to God, shown in good works and love to man. In which of these forms the religious instinct shall be manifested, whether the lowest or the highest, depends, of course, upon the degree of inward culture, and the nature of outward influences. The masters know that the religious instinct of the slave cannot be suppressed, and they seek to divert its manifestation in such way as will least affect the market value of the man. They withhold culture, stifle thought, and feed the religious appetite with dry dogmas and creeds. Of course, the instinct, so confined, can manifest itself only in the lowest form ; and the slave's religion must be such as touches him and his personal welfare, here and hereafter. His God must be personal and mighty ; but not necessarily spiritual and holy. His heaven must be material and gorgeous, but his bare belief must be a ticket of admission. His hell must be very hot for others, but easy of escape for him.

The higher form of manifestation of the religious instinct, in the development of conscience and moral sense, is hardly possible among slaves, except in those rare cases where spontaneous development amounts to moral genius, and makes the man a perfect law unto himself. With an ordinary slave, the moral sense cannot develop itself, and rule the life. Continual fear, and the cravings of ungratified animal instincts, prevent it. He must live, and evade painful work and stripes, rather than not lie. He must have bread enough to eat, rather than not steal it. The denial to him of the natural rights of man prevents any exercise of the correlative duties, and of course any clear understanding of them. Like many free men, the main thing with him is to be right Godward, and with a view to heaven, no matter if he be all wrong *manward ;* and with better reason than others have, because, even without definite consciousness of the fact, he feels that all men are wrong towards him.

As to the highest form of manifestation of the religious instinct, love to God shown in good works and in love to man, it is hardly possible to the ordinary mortal who owns nothing—not even his time, his children, nor himself. With all the lower and selfish propensities and desires for personal happiness thwarted, yet ever craving gratification, how can the higher ones have exercise and growth?

The effect of freedom upon the Canadian refugees has been to lessen the manifestation of the religious instinct in the lower or merely emotional forms, and to increase it in the higher forms of conscience, morality, and good works. Love of God manifests itself less in care about themselves, and anxiety about their own future condition, and more in care for others. Their piety is less nasal, and more practical. They pray less vehemently, but lie and steal less readily. They profess religion less, and practise it more. Here is one instance in which the religious instinct manifested itself in the form of pious work and the performance of duty, rather than in mere emotion and noisy demonstration.

There was a large gathering of colored people at a sort of Methodist love feast to celebrate the completion of a church. The building of the church had been a long and painful business. They had been much perplexed about the ways and means, and each one had exerted himself to the utmost. After the usual prayer and hymn, there was an inspiriting exhortation by the pastor, and then the people were urged "to express themselves." One after another got up and spoke simply and earnestly, but very forcibly; and every one congratulated himself upon having been humbly instrumental in "getting up the church." They thanked God that they had been able to render help in that good work. The pastor, an emotional man, but clearly inferior to many of his flock in point of mind and character, tried hard to stir up some stronger emotion, and to bring out noisy demonstration by interrupting the speakers with "That's right, brother!" "Glory to God!" "Hallelujah!" and the like. But he had no success. The consciousness of good works gave more satisfaction than windy declarations of faith and hope. As a last resort, he struck up

> "John Brown's body lies mouldering in the grave,
> His soul is marching on," &c.

And in this all joined with great enthusiasm; men, women and children shouting out the chorus heartily. The concrete christianity shown in the old hero's self-sacrifice was comprehensible to their religious sense.

Again, their societies for the relief of new comers, or of the feeble and destitute, their private charities, their attentions to the sick, their tributes to the memory of the dead, are all ways through which their religious instincts find gratification in action. If these, or such as these, were wanting, of course the instinct would crave gratification in mere emotional manifestations.

It is further charged, that the slaves are incapable of vital religion, because the most pious of them so frequently lead unchaste lives. But the fountain can rise no higher than its source. The religious instinct of a servile class cannot develop itself in any higher form than that which it assumes in the dominant class, and which governs the relations between them. It cannot be high, if these grow out of low and selfish motives. It cannot be pure, if the relations between the classes are impure. Now, it is notorious, that in one respect, the relation is disgustingly impure. No class with any claim to gentle blood ever so demeaned itself as our slaveholders do. No men, claiming to be gentlemen, ever so defiled themselves.

It is commonly asserted, that in the South, very few white men grow up chaste, and that chastity is unknown among the slaves. This may be exaggerated, but it is certain that the inevitable tendency of American slavery is not only to bring about promiscuous intercourse among the blacks, and between black women and white men, but also to involve white women in the general depravity, and to lower the standard of female purity. Southern gentlemen, and Turkish gentry, both indulging in gross personal licentiousness, think they secure superior virtue among women of their own caste by certain social restraints, and by ferocious vengeance upon the violators of their honor; and both are mistaken. The subject is repulsive, but whoever examines critically the evidence of the social condition of the Slave States, sees that the vaunted superior virtue of Southern women is mere boast and sham.

Nature cannot be cheated; virtue cannot be made to flourish in a vitiated social atmosphere; and it is vitiated through every stratum of slaveholding society. Out of this corrupt community came the crowds of colored refugees within our military lines, who are found to be so grossly dissolute that some good men despair of them, and adopt the slaveholders' doctrine, that the negro is not capable of that moral culture which makes licentiousness seem shocking, and makes personal purity essential to self-respect. But, out of this atmosphere came also the free colored people of the North, who, in spite of political disfranchisement and other disadvantages, already begin to show the effect of breathing a better atmosphere by their growth in moral purity. Out of this atmosphere came also the Canadian refugees, who have already shown that with freedom, and a high social standard before them, they tend upward to virtue as surely as whites do in like circumstances. They show it by setting themselves in families; by respecting the sanctity of marriage; and by general improvement of morals. There are hundreds and hundreds of families whose lives are above reproach. We found there men of natural refinement, living happily and securely in the marriage state, who declared to us that they had always shrunk from the idea of marrying while in slavery, because they could feel no assurance about the previous purity of young women, and no security against forcible violation of their domestic honor.

Treatment of Women.

When freed from the corrupting influences of slavery, the kindly nature of the negro makes him more ready to render justice and respect to woman, than the more selfish nature of the white races allow them to do. The courtesy of the free colored men to their women is well known in the United States; and it is even more marked in Canada. Indeed, the respect paid to women by colored men, as soon as they become free, is one of the most hopeful signs for their race; a sign which the the North American Indians seldom give. A striking instance of this is shown in Liberia. Mr. Cowan met there many whom he had formerly known in Kentucky, and he says there was a change in them for the better. The change was in their manliness, their respect for each other, and "*the respect of the men for the women.*"*

The Constitution of Liberia declares—

> "That the property of which a woman may be possessed at the time of her marriage, and also that of which she may afterwards become possessed, otherwise than by her husband, shall not be held responsible for his debts, whether contracted before or after marriage. Nor shall the property thus intended to be secured to the woman be alienated otherwise than by her free and voluntary consent; and such alienation may be made by her, either by sale or devise, or otherwise."

The Constitution further sets forth, that

> "Adultery, the seduction of a wife or daughter, and the breach of a contract, engagement or promise to marry, are injuries of a peculiar nature, and partake of a criminal character, and actions in regard to them partake of a criminal character."

There is a most interesting fact connected with these provisions. At the instance of the Colonization Society, an eminent jurist† drew up the Constitution for the colonists, and it was sent to Africa, and submitted for their adoption. But the original draft contained none of these provisions securing the rights of women. They were inserted by a committee of colored men in Liberia.

* "Liberia as I Found it." p. 63.

† Professor Greenleaf, of Cambridge, Mass.

GENTLE DISPOSITION OF REFUGEES.

Akin to their religious character, there are certain moral qualities in the negro which are strongly exhibited by the Canadian refugees. Among these are their forgiving tempers, and their affectionate dispositions.

The idea has been advanced in this paper, that the cross between white and negro races serves to lower the tone of the whole animal nature of the progeny, and give less manly force to the intellect than is possessed by either parent race. But whatever may be its effect upon the mental powers, it does not lessen the moral capacities, but, on the contrary, it seems, by softening some of the animal passions, to prepare men for a mission of love. No white race has ever yet learned to turn the unsmitten cheek to the smiter; a black one may. The mulattoes do not show so much ferocity as still lingers in the most civilized white races, and which is sure to burst out when they are hard pushed by oppression or want. It is this lack of ferocity which has enabled the slaveholders to push oppression in some parts of the country to the utmost limit of human endurance, without danger to themselves; for they knew it was the worm and not the adder upon which they trod.

Canada is full of men and women who, in the first half of their lives, were witnesses and sufferers of such indignities and wrongs as would burn into most white men's souls, and make them pass the last half in plotting vengeance. Not so these people. They cherish no spirit of vengeance, and seem to have no grudge against their oppressors. The memory and recital of their wrongs do not arouse such bitter feelings, and call out such maledictions, as would certainly be heard from white men of similar experience.

Only a single instance is recollected in which a feeling of unsatisfied vengeance was manifested; but many could be recalled where the old master and mistress were spoken of with kindness, and a regret expressed that they would not be seen again.

The testimony of Mrs. Wilkinson is a case in point.

"I was raised," said she, "in Winchester, Virginia; I was treated kindly by the Dutchmen with whom I lived, and they freed me after my husband ran away, and gave me my son, when he was about three years old. My husband came here because he wanted to be free. He was not treated right. I was living very well—same as if I was free, although they hadn't given me my free papers. I had no hardships. There were two sets of children, and when the old gentleman was dead, the second set of children thought that they and their mother better give me my freedom and let me go, because, if she died, they didn't know but the first set of children might come in and enslave me. I was twenty-eight years old when I was freed.

"I was over here twenty-one years, and *then went back just to see the old place and all my friends*. That was six years ago. I saw my master's family. I wanted to see them—indeed I did, for I nursed them. I brought them with me, and will get them and show them to you. (Mrs. W. here left the room, and returned presently with a daguerreotype, which she handed to Dr. Howe.) I nursed that man when he was a child. His name is John Hoover. I nursed his brother, too. They thought a good deal of me, and wouldn't do anything at all without asking me. This (another likeness) is a picture of my young master's cousin. She gave it to me herself, thinking I might not go back again, but I don't know but I shall.

"I have seen a good deal of hard treatment of others, but never had any myself. I was just raised up like one of the family. I used to call my master "father," and the old lady "mother," until I came to this country. That is the way I was raised. I came off to follow my husband."

It is remarkable that even the refugees who fled to escape brutal treatment express no dislike to the whites generally. Many often speak of their old mistress with tenderness, and of her children as beloved playmates. Many would like to go back and live in the old place, but never as slaves.

Among the minor virtues of these people is that of

Cheerfulness.

Indeed, the disposition to mirthfulness seems to be so strong in the negro as almost to merit the name of a peculiar quality. Oppression keeps it down for a time; but it continually breaks out in jollity, and there is often more fun and laughter in the cabin than in the master's house. This disposition grows out of their very organization, and their peculiarity in this respect may be among those marvellous arrangements by which Providence prepares races for the parts they are to bear in the drama of existence. Indeed, some physiologists assert that the Caucasian race, during uterine and infantile growth, *passes through* "certain stages of form," which are so much more persistent in the African race as to be characteristic of it. May there not be something akin to this in the moral development of the race? The white man seems to pass out of that phase of young life abounding in mirth and jollity, when he passes beyond boyhood, while the negro remains longer in it, if indeed he ever gets out of it at all. At any rate, the negroes in this country are proverbially mirthful and childish. In the South, they are considered as children, and grown men are called "boys."

But the whole bodily organization and the resulting dispositions are modified by external influences, especially in a cross breed. We have seen how the physical organization of the negroes has been modified at will, and just such kind of men produced as the market demanded. But this is not all. Slavery is instinctively discriminating in the moral, as well as the bodily qualities which it cultivates or represses. The Polish youth in the military schools, established and directed by the dominant Russians, used to assert that while the most rigid military discipline was enforced, and the slightest breach thereof was punished without mercy, moral discipline was not only neglected, but such vices as gambling and licentiousness were encouraged by being merely winked at. A sinful life would make them less likely to be Polish patriots, and more likely to be Russian mercenaries. So, for a slave, mirthfulness is wholesome and harmless; but thinking is dangerous. The one promotes the growth and strength of the body, and that belongs to the master; the other promotes the growth and strength of the soul, and that belongs to the slave.

Moreover, slavery stunts the growth of individuality, and strives to make boyhood lifelong. Of course, there can be no true manliness without the feeling of independent individuality and the habit of self-guidance, and slavery prevents the exercise of these. Then there can be no character without responsibilities and cares, and slaves have few of them. In Canada, the negroes seem to have a more sober aspect. They look older at the same age than slaves do, and are not so rollicking and jolly. This is said doubtingly, because other observers of them say they are more mirthful through life than whites are.

In summing up their moral qualities, it may be said of the Canadian refugees generally, that like the mulattoes of the Northern States, they seem a little effeminate, as though a portion of the *grit* had been left out of their composition. It may be, that with their African blood, they have inherited more of womanly than of manful dispositions; for Africans have more of womanly virtues than fiercer people have. Indeed, it may be said that, among the races, Africa is like a gentle sister in a family of fierce brothers.

General Conclusions, drawn from Observation of the Condition of Colored People of Canada West.

1st. That the negroes of Canada, being for the most part hybrids, are not of robust stock, and are unfavorably affected by the climate; that they are infertile, and their infertility is increased by intermarriage with each other; and therefore, unless their number is kept up by immigrants from the United States, or by some artificial encouragement, they will decrease and disappear in a few generations.

2d. That, with freedom and equality before the law, they are, upon the whole, sober, industrious, and thrifty, and have proved themselves to be capable of self-guidance and self-support.

3d. That they have set themselves in families, and hallowed marriage, whereby sensuality has lessened, and amalgamation between the races nearly ceased.

4th. That they are exceedingly imitative, but incline to imitate what is most worthy of imitation in the society about them, and are decidedly improving in knowledge and virtue.

5th. That those situated upon farms show ability, industry and skill enough to manage them, though their isolation retards their mental improvement.

6th. That when they congregate in large numbers in one locality, and establish separate churches and schools, they not only excite prejudices of race in others, but develop a spirit of caste among themselves, and make less progress than where they form a small part of the local population.

7th. That prejudice against them among the whites (including the English) is engendered by the same circumstances, and manifested with the same intensity, as in the United States.

8th. That they have not taken firm root in Canada, and that they earnestly desire to go to the southern region of the United States, partly from lŏve of warmth, but more from love of *home.*

9th. That, compared with the whites, the per centage of crimes indicative of lax morality is large; that of crimes indicative of malice and ferocity, all things considered, is not large; and that the percentage of pauperism is very small indeed.

10th. That, upon the whole, they promote the industrial and material interests of the country, and are valuable citizens.

General Inferences to be drawn from the experience of Negroes in Canada, as to the probable effect of giving freedom and equality before the law to all Negroes in the United States.

1st. That with freedom and the ownership of property, the instinct of family will be developed, marriages will increase, and promiscuous intercourse decrease. That the tendency of this change to increase population will be more than counteracted by the inferior fertility of the mulatto breed, when not invigorated by crossing with pure types, black or white; so that the colored breed will soon begin to decrease.

2d. That, under freedom, we may safely rely upon the natural laws of affinity to check amalgamation of races, which slavery encourages by putting a premium upon the offspring, and in other ways.

3d. That with entire freedom of movement and security from oppression, much of the colored population of the Northern and Western States will be drawn by the natural laws which govern movements of peoples towards the tropical regions, carrying with them social influences which will soften the ferocity now prevalent, and be beneficial in many respects.

4th. That the negroes of the South are capable of self-guidance and support without other protection than will be needed by poor whites; and that they will be loyal supporters of any government which ensures their freedom and rights.

5th. That when living in communities with whites in not greater proportion than one thousand to fifteen or twenty thousand, antagonism of race will hardly be developed, but the negroes will imitate the best features of white civilization, and will improve rapidly.

6th. That it is not desirable to have them live in communities by themselves.

7th. That they will be docile and easily governed by laws, and however given to petty offences, will not be prone to crimes of grave character; that they will be peculiarly susceptible to religious influence, and excel in some of the Christian virtues.

8th. That they will not be idle, but industrious and thrifty, and that there will be less pauperism among them than is usual among our foreign emigrants.

9th. That by their industry and thrift they will forward the industrial interests of the country, without the fearful demoralization heretofore caused by their oppression and debasement.

Finally, the lesson taught by this and other emigrations is, that the negro does best when let alone, and that we must beware of all attempts to prolong his servitude, even under pretext of taking care of him. The white man has tried taking care of the negro, by slavery, by apprenticeship, by colonization, and has failed disastrously in all; now let the negro try to take care of himself. For, as all the blood and tears of our people in this revolutionary struggle will be held as cheap, if they re-establish our Union in universal freedom, so all the suffering and misery which his people may suffer in their efforts for self-guidance and support will be held cheap, if they bring about emancipation from the control of the whites.

APPENDIX.

[Note, p. 17.]

It was expected that the result of inquiries, instituted, would be known soon enough to enable us to give in this Report a more exact estimate of the population; but it is not. From all information received, however, it appears that the estimate given on p. 17, is not too high.

The following extract from a Report of the School Trustees of the City of London, proves that the census return of that city was entirely wrong; and that probably, the colored people were included in the column of Whites. The Abstract of the Census Report, 1861, states, [page 49,] that there are 35 colored persons in London. But the School Report, dated November, 1862, shows that there were 153 *children*, of whom 96 were of "school age."

"Your Committee have employed careful parties to make an enumeration of the families of colored citizens, the number of children in each family, the number over five years of age, and the number attending school. From the statistics so collected it appears that the whole number of colored families in the city is as follows:—

Ward.	Families.	Number of Children.	Of School Age.	Attending School.
1,	10	23	11	7
2,	0	0	0	0
3,	25	59	36	25
4,	0	0	0	0
5,	11	52	33	18
6,	7	16	14	0
7,	2	3	2	0
	55	153	96	50

Your Committee append, for the inspection of the Board, the lists made out by the enumerators from which the foregoing epitome has been taken, and which shows that the number of colored families in the city is about 55, the number of children 153, of school age 96, and the number attending school 50."

There has been no movement of the population which can by possibility have caused such a change.

[Note No. 2, p. 51.]

Extract from a Report of a Sub-Committee to the school trustees, City of London, November, 1862.

"1. Your Committee are fully satisfied that a feeling is widely diffused among the people, whether well or ill-founded it is useless to inquire, that the negro differs so essentially from the Caucasian race in organic structure, in the effects of climate influences, or both, that any close or intimate relations with them are not desirable. While this feeling exists, while it prevails among the white population to such an extent, it is wrong, it is cruel in us to force their children into the same classes with those of the colored people. Besides, your Committee have seen that the children themselve sympathize in this prejudice of their parents, and manifest a strong dislike to being seated with their colored class-mates; and sometimes this feeling of repugnance is so strongly shown as to require the intervention of the teacher's authority to suppress it. When such is the case, it is vain to expect either harmony or a kindly feeling to prevail in the class-room or play-ground: but rather must we expect to find, on the part of both, a mind predisposed to take and give offence, a bandying of offensive epithets, embittered, acrimonious feelings, and juvenile quarrels. In these petty disputes the parents frequently take part; complaints are made, and will continue to be made by both parties, that their children have been insulted; and, by the colored parents, that theirs have been harshly and perhaps unjustly treated.

There is but little prospect, your Committee fear, of this state of things being remedied while the system of uniting both races in the same classes continues.

2. Your Committee feel it a duty imposed upon them to state plainly—though the task may be an ungracious one—that from some unexplained organic cause, the close proximity of these people, children or adults, is disagreeable to their white neighbors. Your Committee will not be deterred, through any feeling of false delicacy, from stating that, in a close class-room, during the summer months, this effluvium is highly offensive to many of the children, and still more so to many of the teachers. It is very true this cannot be, with any justice, brought against them as a charge for which they are responsible: neither do your Committee wish it, but still they esteem it a powerful reason why a separation should be sought, as the case admits of the application of no other remedy.

3. Your Committee feel convinced that there is, and must be, a want of sympathy between the teacher and this part of her scholars, which is injurious to both. The teacher knows that, in the discharge of her duty, she ought to treat all alike; that she should, without any visible constraint, self-imposed or otherwise, manifest the same affection for one as another. But this she cannot do; and the little colored child feels with disappointment, mingled with grief,

that it has not the same easy access to the heart of the teacher that others of a similar age and character possess. Hence originates the conviction, even when still young, that they are not placed upon the same footing as others. Suspicion is aroused, and they begin to watch with a jealous eye every movement of the teacher, to compare her bearing towards them, the manner in which she recognizes their wish to please and their endeavors to excel, with her bearing and manner in respect to similar conduct on the part of the other children, and draw their own inferences therefrom.

Your Committee are certain that any keen observer can make up his mind upon this part of the subject, in an evening visit to any of the classes where these colored children are most numerous, by observing the different manners in which the two races take leave of the teacher for the day. The beaming eye and radiant smile with which the little white girl approaches her teacher, indicate a warm and assured recognition of her salute; while the little African stands wistfully apart, gazing on the scene, or moves off with either grief, jealousy, or a dogged indifference, visible upon its countenance."

There was much more to this effect; but not one word of censure upon teachers, who by their "*want of sympathy*," proved themselves to be unfit for their duties. A vain effort was made to amend this most discreditable Report, by inserting the following words:—

"That, believing the colored population to be a portion of the human family, who have chosen Canada as the land of their adoption, and being loyal subjects of her Majesty the Queen, we consider them fully entitled to all the civic and religious rights of British subjects, and reject now and henceforth the report of Messrs. Webb, Graydon, &c., which, if ever acted upon, would deny them those equal rights dear to every Briton, and subject them to a great amount of inconvenience and persecution."

The Report was finally amended, by substituting for Section 3d, a less offensive one; but the question of substituting a *caste school* for the common school; of expelling colored children from the common school, and restricting them to the caste school, was settled in the affirmative, by a vote of ten to three. Messrs. Alex. Johnston, McPherson, and Ross, having manliness and pluck enough to vote against the measure, as "Anti-British."

BUXTON SETTLEMENT.

[Abstract of the Testimony of Rev. William King.]

This settlement was formed in 1849. I brought fifteen of my own people here, [slaves whom he had emancipated,] and have trusted to voluntary emigration since. They formed the nucleus of the community, and others came in. In August, 1850, I procured an Act of Incorporation from Parliament. The whole of my plan was this:—

to provide these people with a home, and their children with an education; and with these two things, I felt confident every blessing would come. The men were charged $2.50 an acre for the land, to be paid in twelve annual instalments. When a fugitive came to me who had not a cent, I said to him, "You can go to work, and earn twelve dollars and a half, and pay the first instalment on your land, and have ten years in which to pay the rest." They were all able to pay the first instalment, for the railroads were being built at that time, and they could readily get work. I taught them never to ask for a cent, if they could earn it themselves. You would hardly ever see one of them begging, and we have endeavored to cultivate that principle throughout the whole. They have supplied their own tools and cattle. I was at considerable expense in establishing the settlement, but I have asked no fee or reward, because I knew the moment I did so, it would be said I was acting from mercenary motives. I formed an association, in order to secure all this land, if they failed to purchase it themselves, because I knew speculators would come in and buy it up if I did not take that precaution.

The houses here were put up by the colonists themselves, after a model furnished them, 18 feet by 24, twelve feet high, and set thirty-three feet from the road, and enclosed with a picket fence. In three years after I came here, there were one hundred men who could become British subjects. We can turn out 150 or 160 voters for members of Parliament now, and 220 voters for councillors. I had an anti-alienation clause inserted in the deeds, so that these people could not transfer their land to a white man until they had been here for ten years. That has kept them a compact body, so that the political power they have got will protect them. Prejudice has melted before that political power, and now the people are respected and elected to office—path-masters, school trustees, and councillors. That is as high as we can get; for a white man would never vote for a colored man as member of Parliament. In this district, we have had two Councillors in one year.

At the present time, two thousand acres are deeded, in fee simple, one-third of which has been paid for, principal and interest. The whole block contains nine thousand acres. The population of the settlement is about one thousand—men, women, and children. I have made them self-supporting in all material matters, and they are more than half self-supporting in their schools at the present moment. They have established two schools in the northern part of the settlement, of which they pay all the expenses, and as soon as I can get them to pay for the land, I shall make this school [the central] self-supporting. The most that any of them owe on fifty acres of land is $183. I expect to settle the whole thing up in eighteen months. I have no doubt in regard to their paying every cent on their land. I am making arrangements to get all the deeds out this fall, and let them borrow the money from a money-lender and pay what is due, giving him mortgages, which I am sure will all be paid in eighteen months. They are apt to take advantage when they find they are not compelled by necessity to pay what they owe. Out of all who came in, there were only three who had their first instalment paid by a friend. I took the notes of the three parties for the amount; one of them paid, but the others will not. If the friend who advanced the money had been a Jew, they would have paid him. I have known some of the men to borrow a hundred dollars for their own purposes, and it has always been repaid.

From the day I came here to this, there has not been a drunken colored man in this settlement. No man is allowed to sell liquor in this settlement; and to the honor of the people be it said, that when one man came on our borders and opened a grog-shop, he could not remain twelve months, for they would not support him. But if brought together, and left to idleness, they would soon become demoralized.

With regard to the climate, I find that when the colored people are clothed the same as Canadians, it has no more influence on them than on whites. Those I brought from Louisiana stood the climate just as well as those who were born in the North. In general, they are quite robust and healthy. There has been but very little sickness in the settlement. We have had no epidemic. We vaccinate the people, and have had but one case of small-pox.

There are some large families here. There is one man with fourteen children; another has twelve; another, ten. They are about half blacks and half mulattoes. The average of children to a family is about three, —not including the deaths. I don't think the mortality here has been any greater than it would have been in any settlement, under the same circumstances. I think the mulattoes are not so long-lived here as the whites or the blacks. And even in New Orleans, Dr. Stone—very good authority there—stated to me that he was of opinion that the mixed race would die out in four generations. I have watched that matter since, and it seems to me that, as a class they have not the same stamina as pure blacks or pure whites.

Only four illegitimate children have been born in this settlement; and that is a better state of things than you will find in Europe. In England, Scotland, or Ireland, the proportion of bastards is much greater. The people here consider it a disgrace. I observe that they pay a very great respect to chastity and to the marriage relation. They all want to be proclaimed in church three times. There will be cases of infidelity among them, but the guilty parties are not respected. The most blame falls on the woman. Very few cases of adultery have come under my observation. I strongly suspect three or four women, from their conduct among men; but I have no proof of their criminality.

We have had one or two cases of petty larceny, and one of manslaughter. The class we have here has been very free from pilfering; it has been an exception to the generality of the race. I will tell you one fault they have; when they borrow an article from me, they never return it. I cannot say they have stolen it; but they neglect to return it.

If freedom is established in the United States, I don't think it will have any effect upon the settlers here; but the young men and young women who are educated here will go down there, because they cannot get white schools here to teach, such is the prejudice against them, and there are not colored schools enough to employ them. I don't think colored schools will be multiplied here, because they are not expedient, and in a few years I think there will be but few left in the Province. I have never encouraged the formation of villages, because I thought the mainstay of the people would be agriculture. If any of the settlers are unfortunate, the others freely help him. There are thirty orphans in the settlement, who are supported by different families.

This settlement is a perfect success; there is no doubt about that. I am prepared to prove that in any place. Here are men who were bred in slavery, who came here and purchased land at the government prices, cleared it, bought their own implements, built their own houses after a model, and have supported themselves in all material circumstances, and now support their schools, in part. I charge them twenty-five cents a month for schooling, when they are able to pay it. Not one-fourth pay here, where there is no compulsion; but in the government schools, where the law obliges them to do so, they all pay it. I consider that this settlement has done as well as any white settlement would have done, under the same circumstances; and I am prepared to prove that a colored community can be made industrious and self-supporting, if they are properly treated. I have no doubt that the colored people of your country, as soon as the war is over, if they are put upon the farms of the South, will become self-supporting. A finer class of laborers cannot be found in the world for raising cotton. Only introduce Northern capital, or Southern capital, give them full remuneration, and in a short time you will find them an industrious, respectable, self-supporting community.

www.ingramcontent.com/pod-product-compliance
Lightning Source LLC
LaVergne TN
LVHW021428110826
845150LV00007B/2130

9781425507435